Ele Jane
2017

WHEN WEAK, THEN STRONG

Disability in the life of the Church

D1685064

Faith Bowers

Bloomsbury Central Baptist Church
on behalf of BUild
2008

Published by Bloomsbury Central Baptist Church
235 Shaftesbury Avenue, London WC2H 8EL
on behalf of BUild - the Baptist Union initiative with people
who have learning disabilities

Printed by Tyndale Press (Lowestoft) Ltd

ISBN 978-0-9530341-2-3

Cover picture: Vivian Cheng

Dedicated
to
Doris Barrera

A Chilean Baptist with a promising career in music, Doris saw how music therapy helped her nephew who has severe learning disabilities. She decided to devote her gifts to children with special needs. Coming to London to train in 2007, she had an horrific traffic accident. Her determined and cheerful courage, ready smile and firm faith, while coming to terms with chronic pain and long-term disability, have been an inspiration to all in Bloomsbury Central Baptist Church. In her life this young woman reflects many of the concerns covered in this book.

WHEN WEAK, THEN STRONG
Disability in the life of the Church

Contents

WHEN WEAK,
THEN STRONG

To keep me from being unduly elated by the magnificence of such revelations, I was given a thorn in my flesh, a messenger of Satan sent to buffet me; this was to save me from being unduly elated. Three times I begged the Lord to rid me of it, but his answer was: 'My grace is all you need; power is most fully seen in weakness.'

I am therefore happy to boast of my weaknesses, because then the power of Christ will rest upon me. So I am content with a life of weakness, insult, hardship, persecution, and distress, all for Christ's sake; for when I am weak, then I am strong.

Paul of Tarsus
2 Corinthians 12:7-10 (REB)

Many people who have a serious disability know quite a lot about insults, hardship, distress and often even persecution. Some rage against this injustice, but there are those who learn to be content with a life of weakness and in that discover an inner strength. Often this overflows to become a strength for others too.

This book is a combined revision of two earlier books, *Complete in Christ* (BUGB 1996) and *Treat with special honour* (BUGB 1997), dealing respectively with the place of people who have physical and learning disabilities in the life of the Christian church.

The title is taken from Joel 3.10, echoed in 2 Corinthians 12.10, and again in the chorus of the worship song, 'Give thanks with a joyful heart':

> Let the weak say, 'I am strong',
> let the poor say, 'I am rich,
> because of all the Lord has done for me'.
> Give thanks.

This sums up what the network known as BUild - *the Baptist Union initiative with people with learning disabilities* - is all about: enabling people to get a fresh perspective on their disabilities as they experience the fullness of life in Christ.

Whenever I hear that song, I am taken back to a BUild conference years ago when worship was led by a youth who had recently come to personal faith. Like many with Down's Syndrome, he was short in stature and could only just be seen as he stood behind the lectern. He wore hearing aids and thick lenses, but his voice rang out with cheerful confidence as he introduced his choice of final song: 'Let the weak say, "I am strong"'.

BUild is primarily concerned with learning disabilities, but those involved are well aware of physical disabilities too, since learning disability is often accompanied by physical and/or sensory disabilities. The term *developmental disabilities,* used in America, conveys better the package of impaired abilities that often go together.

Looking at physical and learning disabilities in a single book, however, presents a difficulty, because most people with a physical or sensory disability are not impaired in intellect and may be sensitive about any implied connection. Here, however, the focus is on *enabling* people. The nature of various disabilities is discussed only to help churches address those things that can help to reduce the problems caused by various impairments.

The World Health Organization in 1980 defined *impairment* as any loss or abnormality of structure or function, *disability* as a restriction resulting from an impairment, and *handicap* as the disadvantage to an individual resulting from an impairment or disability. This book, however, draws considerably on the experience of people of goodwill who do not always use 'politically correct' terminology. Moreover, some quotations were gathered some years ago and, while the points they make remain valid, some use 'handicap' more widely for disability. Even now, in 2008, the language of impairment has not penetrated far into everyday usage. People have caught on more to the concept of being 'challenged' in some way - visually challenged, height challenged. etc. - but that is because it lends itself to funny variations, like 'follically challenged' for bald. What matters more is the attitude behind the words. One of the most inclusive remarks made to my son came when he was teasing a girl as the youth club gathered for a camping trip. Laughing she gave him a friendly shove, 'You are an idiot, Richard!' It was once the technical term for such a person, but she was treating him just as she would any of the boys.

Recent legal requirements insist that public buildings, churches included, address access. Important here are the Disability Discrimination Acts of 1995 and 2005. There are also more stringent requirements over accounting, health and safety, the protection of children and vulnerable adults, and catering standards: churches must take all this on board. Requirements which are basically good have costly implications, and it can be difficult, especially for smaller churches, to find suitable personnel to monitor them all. It is easy to resent access requirements, especially if the church does not see anyone who will obviously benefit from a ramp or whatever.

Nevertheless, good provision can be good for outreach: there is a mission perspective to this.

It is possible to do all the right things to the building yet still not have a positive attitude towards people who live with disabilities. It is possible to ensure good access for wheelchairs to every part of the premises but still be totally unaware of smaller things that could make a difference to people with other disabilities.

This book is not, however, just about the nature of disabilities and possible aids. It is more about recognizing that God loves us all, just as we are, and that disability is not in itself a barrier to faith. Disabilities do not necessarily impair spirituality. When it comes to Christian service, disabilities will increase the effort needed but not preclude the possibility of contributing to the life of the church.

The book is about liberating people to serve the Lord. People who know where their disabilities present particular problems in church life have offered down-to-earth, practical advice about ways churches and friends could make life a bit easier for others like them. It is not so much about the clinical conditions that cause impairment but about how people cope with their particular difficulties and endeavour to live to the full, sustained by the Lord whose body was broken for them. Many would never draw attention to these matters on their own behalf but have been persuaded to speak out for the sake of others with similar disabilities.

As I first compiled this material, listening to many people with first-hand experience of disability, I came to feel, perhaps to my surprise at the time, that Complete in Christ was really about discipleship, as people found how they could offer their gifts into the life of the church. Treat with special honour I increasingly saw as a book about evangelism, both as churches found fresh ways to present the Gospel in the face of communication difficulties, but also as Christians with severe learning disabilities found their own ways of making the good news in Christ known to others.

Let the weak say, 'I am strong!'

Acknowledgements

Mrs Joyce Costie a member of Grangetown Baptist Church in Cardiff, prompted me to compile this material. She was born with multiple disabilities but these never prevented her from being an active disciple of Christ. Her essay on 'The Churches' Response to Disabilities', written as part of her work for the Baptist Union's Christian Training Programme Diploma, provided core material. Her undiminished zest for life and joy in her faith, and her lack of resentment, either over her disabilities or the inadequacies of others, provided the initial inspiration for this book.

Mrs Costie herself acknowledges the help she received with her original project from the Cardiff Institute for the Blind, the Royal National Institute for the Blind, Cardiff Torch Fellowship, Church Action on Disability, Christian Disabled Fellowship, South Glamorgan Social Services, National Deaf Blind League, Sense Cymru, Macular Disease Society and the Partially Sighted Society.

Part 2 draws heavily on members of the BUild network, especially David Buckingham, Tim Burt, David Clark, Siôr Coleman, Jackie Colgrove, Alison Gidney, Sue Houghton, Gary Knott, Pat Maisch, Sally Nelson, Jerry Newsome, Joan Riley, Barbara Stanford, Audrey Saunders, John Williams, Patricia Wiltshire, and Susan Wright.

Thanks are also due to Sheila Ashe, Miriam Barker, Eileen Bebbington, Brian Bowers, Grace Carter, Michael Cleaves, Iain Collins, Barbara Crowe, Sue Fifield, Liz Fleming, Ruth Gouldbourne, Hazel

Greenwood, John Harden, Carol Harvey, Elizabeth Heap, Trish Howse, Paul Jackson, Margaret Jarman, Margaret Johns, Christopher Lee, Betty Leech, Craig Millward, Peter Manson, Giles and Derek Murray, Liz Neal, Sally Nelson Dennis Nolan, Joan Norton, Edmund and Ann Palmer, Dorothy Pracy, Walter Ractliffe, Ena Robertson, Rosemarie Sims, Paul Smith, Clive Tibbles, Ann Tooke, Edna Weir, Paul Weldon and others who preferred not to be named. Several of these have since died, but their words of experience and wisdom remain valid. Many informal conversations over the years have also fed into the work. Vivian Cheng kindly agreed to the use on the cover of her picture, originally a contribution to Lenten worship in the Bloomsbury church.

The work of Causeway Prospects, the sessions they have run at Springharvest, and the worship and teaching materials they produce have led a number of churches to begin special ministries with those who have learning disabilities. Their resources can be found on their website.

I particularly wish to thank friends who have learning disabilities for insights I have received from them, especially Richard Bowers, Verna Carter, Grant Connelly, Robert Dunham, Sarah Gilbert, Dawn Henshaw, Pamela James, Philip May, Sue Norris, Michael Roberts, Viv Simmonds, Brian Smithson, Alison Taylor, David Teague, Debbie Wiles and Mark Williams.

Faith Bowers
9 August 2008

Part 1

COMPLETE IN CHRIST
People with physical disabilities in the life of the Church

The Nature of Physical Disability

Within the Bible we find people with physical disabilities - blind, lame, paralysed, disease-damaged - they are all there. Many experience miraculous healing, especially those who come into direct contact with Jesus. Miracles can and do still happen, occasionally with dramatic suddenness, often more slowly and worked through the skill of doctor and surgeon. My husband assures me that careful explanation of the process of cataract removal in no way lessens the miracle of lost sight restored. Nevertheless, most people with a severe disability are stuck with it for life: for them, healing and wholeness are about accepting this, coming to terms with it, and allowing themselves to develop and grow on that apparently unpromising soil.

The apostle Paul, great in faith and greatly used by God, had his 'thorn in the flesh'. He does not tell us what this was, but, in spite of repeated prayer, he was not cured of this infirmity. He had to live with it, and through it learned more about God's grace and the divine paradox of power most fully seen in weakness. Here is encouragement for those who continue to bear their Christian witness while struggling with disabling conditions.

We tend to assume that disability is quite rare. In most churches a few people will easily be identified as 'disabled'. Almost certainly others will have some significant disability, probably only apparent to those who know them well. Some can keep their disability secret - perhaps partly by restricting their activities. In reality, a sizeable section of the population lives with significant disability. In Britain the figure is about one in seven with a disability, while one in four are close to someone with a disability.

'People want disability to be simple', observed a blind man on the radio, but it is *not*. There can be great variety of effect, even with a single type of disability. Each individual is different. The best guide, therefore, to advise on how to help will be the one who has the disability, though often that person will need sensitive encouragement to offer that advice. Considering a range of disabilities and indicating the kind of consideration or provision that may help should equip friends to be more sensitive to the possibilities. A short book cannot cover every possibility but should help people be more aware of the difficulties others may experience, particularly in the context of church life. Positive attitudes and practical aids can help people experience more completely the joy and responsibility of being members of the body of Christ.

People's attitudes to their disabilities vary. I have dared to edit this book because I have lived with and loved three men with disabilities. Each reacted differently. My father, suddenly blinded in mid-life and soon unable to walk because of multiple sclerosis, never came to terms with this. He raged against his infirmity and neither family, friends nor faith could prevent his last years from being pretty miserable. My husband, with a 'hidden' disability from his youth, has determinedly got on with life, making light of his limitations. Over the years he has reluctantly accepted that it is easier if friends and colleagues understand - though would still rather his wife did the explaining. My son has little resentment of his learning disability but can be quick to capitalize on it, enlisting help and ever alert to claim any concessions going. None of these attitudes is unique. As increasing age affects my own mobility, I have become more aware both of the nuisance and of the amount of goodwill around as people leap to offer a seat or point out the lift.

Most people want to be kind and helpful, but the help they offer can be inappropriate if the needs are not properly understood. Uninformed kindness often results in an embarrassing fuss. Most people with disabilities prefer help to be as unobtrusive as possible. Genuine love demands sensitive awareness. A caring church can reduce the problems and thereby release into church and world the gifts and abilities too easily trapped within people because of disabling conditions.

Christian love ought to be reason enough to learn how to help, but there are likely to be immediate rewards for the church that is open to people who have disabilities. I remember a young father, an able professional man but severely crippled with arthritis, who was joint church secretary with a colleague who had a speech defect. He told us, 'I can't walk and she can't talk, but between us we can do the job!' That said a lot about the will to serve of that man and that woman, but it also said something about the church that saw in its midst two *able* people.

Material here comes from those who know what it is really like. All the contributors are believing, active Christians who usually prefer to focus as little as possible on their disabilities. I have been touched by their willingness to share private feelings and perceptions when persuaded that this could help others. I have been repeatedly moved by their strong faith in God.

Joyce's Story

Joyce Costie was born in London in 1927. Short-sighted and squinting from birth, she wore spectacles from the age of nine months. A serious throat condition prevented her from feeding normally and required surgery and speech therapy. She grew no first teeth and her second teeth only came after her gums were cut - and were then so crooked she had to wear a brace long before the fashion for widespread orthodontics.

My early days were spent in and out of hospitals, unable to see, speak or walk properly. What life was there for me - helpless, hopeless and useless? In those days [such] children were put into an Institution. This was during the years of depression, means tests, and redundancy before World War II.

When Joyce was five, measles struck the family. All five brothers, including her twin, died within a month. 'It meant a lot of saving and having to go without to pay for five funerals.' The two sisters survived, but further damage was done to Joyce's already poor sight, hearing, balance and limb control. She remembers vividly:

... the frustration of not being able to use my limbs as a child ... of being taken to school, standing against a wall watching other children doing things. Then getting very frustrated at the eye hospital because I could not do the exercises, like trying to get the lion into the cage - sometimes seeing two lions and no cages, then vice versa. The frustrations of being unable to pick myself up after losing my balance ... of not being able to hear in church, not being able to see the hymn-books clearly ... I could not do anything, except get very frustrated and irritable because I could not do anything.

Joyce needed surgery to give her any chance of a normal life, but the loving parents who chose to keep this disabled child within the family could not afford treatment in those pre-NHS days. Then a miracle happened: 'A gentleman brought his son into the hospital for an operation, and paid for his son to have it, he also paid for mine.' That operation was the great turning-point. Joyce was effectively given new life 'because a gentleman paid the price! I never met this gentleman, I do not know his name or address so could not visit him to thank him. I know about him and can speak about him and what he did many years ago, but I do not know him personally.' Joyce compares this with her experience of Christ.

Her biggest immediate need had been met, but traumas of war beset her later childhood. She was 'evacuated somewhere on the south coast, then when things began to hot up, re-evacuated somewhere else. Then we were bombed out, my parents moved to Dorset. I got a job in Salisbury. During all this time I went to Sunday School with my sister and church with my sister and parents. I was baptized in 1941 in Northcote Road Baptist Church because Battersea Chapel was bombed.' The family worshipped for a time at Bloomsbury, where Joyce, the girl once unable to speak, sang in the choir. In Salisbury she joined Brown Street Baptist Church.

As a young woman, Joyce was fit enough to work in the Middle East for ten years, in Egypt, Cyprus, Benghazi, Tripoli, Jerusalem and Malta. Wherever she went, she was active in the church, helping with Sunday School, Brownies and Guides, and leading Bible Studies.

She married and settled in Cardiff in 1967. Soon she was in demand there as a speaker at Sisterhoods and Women's Meetings, and often led Bible Studies and Prayer Meetings. In spite of continuing health problems, she became the Grangetown Missionary Secretary and area representative for the Women's World Day of Prayer. In 1980 she developed breast cancer and subsequent lymphatic disorder, yet six months after the mastectomy she was inducted as President of the Cardiff and District Women's Missionary Association. In 1987 she was President of the Cardiff and District Baptist Missionary Auxiliary.

In 1991 Joyce realized her sight, hearing and balance were all deteriorating. She was told she would go blind, but still have enough sight 'to go from A to B'. 'In my frustration I said, "but I want to go from A to G!" Her doctor replied, 'You can go from A to B, then C, then D, and get to G eventually. Don't be in such a hurry!' She began to learn Braille, 'because I wanted to know yesterday what I can do today to prepare for tomorrow.'

Joyce lost the central vision in both eyes. The right could still make out a little in the distance, the left could read large print with a low vision aid (glasses which block the other eye and magnify powerfully for the 'reading' eye). She could still manage a hymn book but had to keep swapping her glasses over during a worship service.

Frustrated when she could not longer hear the sermon, she enquired about lip reading, but her sight ruled this out. The RNID adviser introduced her to the neck loop system, connecting the church loudspeaker directly to her own amplifier. So, she wrote, 'I sit at the front of the church tethered to a loudspeaker with a noose around my neck!'

Widowed and with her senses all failing, Joyce has often felt down, but at her lowest ebb she has seen visions and dreamed dreams in which the Light of the World penetrates her darkness, strengthening her faith and renewing her irrepressible hope.

My problems are small compared to others. I do have a visual impairment ... a hearing loss ... a balance problem. I don't have a sense of taste or smell and, as someone said, I seem to miss an awful lot in life - but not as much as others.

This remarkable lady persisted through the ten years of failing health it took her to complete that CTP Diploma in her desire to equip herself to proclaim Christ more effectively. That in turn brought her new opportunities for Christian service through spoken and written word.

With age, Joyce developed osteoporosis and arthritis of the jaw. One letter reported that she could no longer yawn or chew - but was still able to undertake speaking engagements.

At the age of 79, she had a change of consultant. The new doctor found he could restore some clarity to her limited vision. 'This', she wrote, 'has turned my life right round'.

Reading Joyce's story, and reading her cheerful letters in which that indomitable spirit always provides something that makes me laugh, I think of Charles Wesley's verse:

> Hear him, you deaf; his praise, you dumb,
> your loosened tongues employ.
> You blind, behold you Saviour come,
> and leap, ye lame, for joy!

Perceptions of Disability

All people, whatever their abilities or disabilities, should have the opportunity to hear the Gospel. We have the responsibility and privilege of making sure that none are deprived of this because of poor provision for the disabled. There is so much that all can be actively involved in if given opportunity to use their talents for the Lord's work in the church and the community. Once it is made possible for them to join in, people with disabilities may partake in many of the normal activities of a church: lead Bible studies, join in prayer groups, sing in the choir, edit church magazines.

Thus writes Joyce. At a conference on disability, she was struck by a church secretary remarking, 'We are all well in our church so we just do not give it a thought till it comes our way and we don't know what to do'. It will be a rare church indeed where all are fully able. One suspects that a church apparently without disabled people must either be so insensitive that it discourages them from coming or so quietly aware that good provision reduces the problems so no-one stands out as disabled.

Encouraging people with certain disabilities to be part of the fellowship may highlight the need for first-aiders, but an accident or emergency can occur anywhere anytime. It is a good idea to identify two or three people who know what to do in case of accidents, sudden collapse or fits. Some congregations are well provided with medical personnel, others may need to identify willing people and seek first-aid training. This is usually locally available, e.g. from the Red Cross or St John's Ambulance.

Disability is not simple and problems do not always come singly. Those affected from birth often have multiple disabilities in parallel, and old age often adds to existing ones, or brings several to people previously able-bodied.

Nevertheless, people with a variety of different disabilities mention a number of common factors. If we grasp these recurrent themes, we shall lay some foundation before looking in more detail at some disabling conditions.

Disability is embarrassing

Many people mention the embarrassment - either over the disability itself or over asking for special consideration which draws attention to the disability. Most try to keep the disability as unobtrusive as possible: it is not what they want others to notice about them!

Which of us is not tempted to look twice at someone who is different? That second glance may be sympathetic - we may be wondering whether there is anything we may do to help - but we are still noticing the *condition* rather than the *person*. I observed the guide dog's harness as the blind man took the seat opposite me on the underground train. I registered alertness to help if needed, but it was only when I saw the portcullis logo on his Braille papers that I recognized the MP's face, familiar from television.

The person who bears some mark of disability always thinks its 'oddness' stands out a mile, though it may be barely noticeable to passers-by. Try going out in two unmatched shoes: most people will not notice, yet to the wearer it feels as though everyone is staring.

One contributor said he 'used to find children the hardest to cope with - they are unashamedly honest. But now I find that I'd rather cope with answering a straight question from a child than the embarrassed and hushed response from a parent.' A neighbouring four-yearold came to play with my preschool son. After a while she came to me earnestly: 'Is there something wrong in Richard's head so he cannot talk properly or is he just being silly?' 'There is something wrong.' 'That's all right then' and she ran back happily to her playmate, leaving me wishing I found it that easy to accept.

When it comes to practical assistance, there is always a delicate balance between what is helpful and what makes the disability more conspicuous. Friends who know about particular difficulties can be alert to ensure that suitable provision is quietly made and so avert embarrassment. Discover and respect personal preferences. Everyone is different and would-be helpers should find out what is best for that person - sensitively, since the disabled person may not find it easy to talk about this.

Some time after compiling the first edition of this book, I led a weekend for a church wanting a focus on disability. On the Sunday morning I preached from John's account (chapter 9) of Jesus healing the blind man and all the questions that followed. At the door afterwards I realized that for that morning at least disability had, unusually, become an acceptable subject. Almost everyone as they left wanted to speak of their own experience of disability. For some, it was their own disability, obvious or unseen; for others, it was an experience, past or present, within their family or through a close friend. This was an ordinary, typical-looking congregation, and it reminded us just how common is serious disability. For a little while, that morning, it had become a socially acceptable subject.

Disability breeds false assumptions

It is not just a matter of being *seen* as different: problems also lie in the assumptions others make on the basis of what they see. People observe a disability and assume it affects more of the person than is really the case, often imagining that the mind, as well as the body, will be impaired. Physical and learning disabilities do sometimes occur together, but that should never be assumed. Neither will all those who have the same condition be affected in identical ways. There may be some common features but stereotyping is unhelpful: focus rather on the individual. Disabled people come in all sorts ad conditions, with different backgrounds and interests, different characters and temperaments - just like the able-bodied. Above all, we should be careful not to impose restrictive human ideas on what it means to be made in the image of God.

Underlying all that is contained in this book, and surely underlined by faith in a personal Saviour, is this primary need to relate to the individual and not to be blinded by the disability. Blindness begins with making false assumptions and it happens so 'naturally' that we fall into the trap without realizing. Goodwill is not enough - we have to work at this deliberately if we are to be properly aware and enabling.

A minister whose body is visibly 'different' observes, 'I hate the almost weekly look of surprise (almost entirely amongst church folk) when they discover I am a minister. It betrays all their assumptions and is very hard to bear.'

An undergraduate with cerebral palsy had always found the church welcoming and loving, apparently without reservations - until she fell in love with a ministerial student. Then

> very many older Christians took it upon themselves to make it clear to us that it could not possibly be God's will for a minister to marry someone with a physical handicap. I was thunderstruck. I knew the Lord had accepted me and I could not understand why his people should not. And yet these were mature Christians who were telling us we were wrong

... We both grew up a lot, emotionally and spiritually, over the course of the next few months, when we prayed and talked and prayed again, and eventually accepted that we were not going our own way and disregarding the leading of the Spirit, but that our marriage was indeed his plan for us.

God's vision went far beyond that of their anxious Christian friends. Their partnership strengthened her husband in ministry and one of their daughters is also a Baptist minister.

Disability is time-consuming

Many people with severe disabilities manage to live remarkably normal lives, but it is always at the expense of considerable time and effort. A woman with a responsible professional job and paralysed legs once told me, 'If *you* ladder your nylons just as you are going out, it is an irritating nuisance. If *I* do, I have to get back on to the bed and it takes me twenty minutes to change them.' How early did she have to get up to be in the office at 9 a.m.? She and her husband, both using wheelchairs, still found time to give to church work.

Most disabilities make some everyday activities take longer. It is good to bear this in mind - though those affected may well make light of it.

Disability makes life harder all round

Many disabled people are further disadvantaged by constraints on employment and on income, insurance, mortgage and pension provision. All this adds to the anxieties, especially for those with dependent families.

A family with a severely disabled member will have less corporate spare time and energy for those extra domestic jobs, like gardening and decorating, and probably less money to pay to have work done. My mother injured her back lifting my paralysed and incontinent father. A home-help came three mornings a week. Our parents grieved that their two schoolgirl daughters had much more than homework to do in evenings and weekends. The garden was a worry - we needed the vegetables and fruit but not the work! Occasionally a former colleague of my father's would do a bit of digging, but we had to cope with the rest. One spring day the men of the church organized a working party to get the garden under control for us. They even rigged lights in the trees to continue as dusk fell. Our memory of that happy day is doubtless clearer because this was an isolated event - in the seven years of my father's illness.

If someone is too disabled to be left alone, that is hard for the family too. My mother taught evening classes, when we could be home to look after our father. The evening carer had to concentrate on homework to the accompaniment of radio or talking book.

Precious are those friends who visit regularly, enriching the disabled person's life and releasing carers to do something outside the home. In days when family vehicles were rarer, our church secretary had the smallest car of any around the congregation and the most duties on Sundays, but he proved the dependable friend who took my father and his wheelchair to church in that tiny Austin, while his wife and sons walked. Oliver was also responsible for my father's happiest days, when county cricket came to the local ground. He would gallantly push the wheelchair across the grass and provide a running commentary. The blind man revelled in the atmosphere and sound of bat on ball. We learned a lot about self-giving, Christlike love from that apparently stern schoolmaster and his generous family.

Care for the Carers

While the primary focus of this book is on those who themselves have serious disabilities, churches should also be aware of those who care for them. Often this will be family members, but many people are involved in care. Many fine carers in Britain today are drawn from the immigrant population, because it is work that can be done with limited command of English and where a few hours a week can be fitted around studies where visas only permit strictly limited earnings. Churches ought to be aware who in their midst give care, whether within families or as paid carers. Similarly there may be members involved in various professions, in health, education or social services, that seek to help people with disabilities. It is good to recognize all those who work on behalf of others in need.

According to the 2001 Census one person in twelve in England and Wales provides unpaid care for a family member or friend. Over a million provide care for more than fifty hours per week. Many of these full-time carers are themselves elderly and not in good health. Others provide this care in addition to their paid employment.

Carers often feel isolated. They are tied to the care situation, and anyway they are too exhausted for much social life.

Even with the relative normality of a young child who just seemed younger than his actual age. I remember feeling somehow apart from the other mothers collecting preschoolers from the Play Group. We were not invited to their afternoon get-togethers in the park or tea-parties. I was not asked to join the committee or fund-raising activities. This was in marked contrast to experience at the gate of my elder son's primary school. But that is as nothing compared with the isolation of many mothers with far more severely disabled children.

This sense of being different makes parents extra sensitive. They can be hurt by attitudes to them and to those they care for.

Sometimes even kindly-meant but thoughtless remarks sting. It helps when friends offer practical and prayer support.

Those responsible for pastoral care in the church will be alert to parents' needs at the time of initial diagnosis, whether at birth or later. They ought also to be especially alert to the stress on parents at times of transition, when difficult choices have to be made. Some of these will relate to medical tests and assessments. Some will relate to beginning school and changing schools. Some will come when the child grows up and there are questions about the care and placement of the adult son or daughter. Mothers who have devoted their lives to caring for a disabled child, with no question of picking up their career once babyhood was past, will not find 'letting go' that easy.

Letting go can take various forms. It may mean entrusting the full-time care of a wholly dependent child to others. It may be about allowing a relatively able child to become more independent - for us the biggest challenge was letting our son travel on his own. The magnitude will vary but in all cases it will be a stressful time and sensible, sympathetic support will be valued.

Sally Nelson described in the *Baptist Ministers' Journal*, October 2002, what caring for her daughter with multiple disabilities entails:

In the year 2001 we kept 90 appointments for her ... a punishing schedule of referrals, therapy sessions and medical investigations...

It is very hard from the outside to understand the extra pressures of a child with special needs because all (particularly young) children are demanding, but the problems may not be obvious. For example, back pain is now part of my life: simple things like lifting our child into her car seat are difficult now she weighs one-third of my adult weight. We can never let go of her hand when out, in case she falls over. She cannot dress herself because she cannot balance. Daily life adds up to a big logistical exercise.

User-friendly Premises

Right attitudes come first and can smooth the way over many practical difficulties, yet the immediate environment is important. Many church buildings are old, built when disabled people were rarely seen in public. They may have steps, narrow aisles, awkward pews, pillars partially blocking the way, all creating difficulties for wheelchair users and even for those who just need a walking stick. Doors may not be wide enough, and toilets awkward (assuming they are provided at all). Yet, where there is the will, it is usually possible to adapt older buildings to improve access.

Newer buildings should have been designed with some consideration for better access. Current legislation requires public buildings, churches included, to make proper provision for those with mobility and other disabilities. This can be expensive and may be seen as an unwelcome extra burden, but good access speaks volumes about a welcoming church and can open doors for the Gospel.

Not just the main worship area but church halls and the approaches to smaller rooms need attention so that people with disabilities can join in social functions, prayer meetings, Bible studies, committee meetings and fellowship groups during the week.

In existing buildings much can be done to increase safety, dignity and independence. Hand-rails make steps safer: remember that people's weaker side varies so there really needs to be a rail on each side of steps, or one up the middle that can be used from either side. Reasonably high seats with fixed arms help people get up and down unaided. In the modern kitchen streamlined worktops are normally at standing height: one lower worktop or table with knee-room below for those who need to sit enables more to share in the work and the fellowship that goes with it. This applies not only to people using wheelchairs but to the many who find prolonged standing difficult.

A Check-List

1. All steps, inside and outside, should be edge-marked with a contrast strip.
2. Hand-rails, both left and right, should be provided for all steps.
3. There should be alternative access by ramp.
4. Doorways should be wide to allow comfortable wheelchair access.
5. Space for wheelchairs should be made in the body of the congregation (not only at front or back).
6. Suitable toilets should be provided - with wide doors and grab-rails, and no steps.
7. Good lighting is important.
8. Induction loop systems should be fitted.
9. Large print hymn-books/sheets should be readily available.
10. Braille Bibles and hymn books should be provided.
11. Make photocopies in large print available. Braille copies of anything shown on screen may also be required.
12. Church notice boards should be at eye level for maximum legibility.
13. Have Sign interpreters and provision for lip-reading for the profoundly deaf.
14. Identify First Aiders - if necessary, get some trained.

The sections that follow explain some of these in more detail.

NB *Where such provision is made, it is worth advertizing the fact. Good practice can be part of the church's outreach: it proclaims that all are welcome here.*

Some Conditions

There are many support bodies relating to different disabilities. Today the best way to find up-to-date information on these will be to look up the condition on the web. When someone is newly given a diagnosis, church friends may be able to help them find sources of information, help and support.

The best person to tell you what would be most helpful to anyone who has a disability in your church will normally be that individual, or the family or carers. Where it is a child with disabilities, bear in mind that not only parents but also brothers and sisters may be a useful source of information. Some children are very good at discovering the interests of a child who is a bit different and helping them join in more.

The material that follows, relating to a number of disabling conditions, draws on the experience of people who know about them 'from the inside'. This is not a comprehensive survey, but we have tried to reach beyond the usual disability concerns, sometimes summed up as 'ramps, loops and loos', to alert readers to the wide range of possible disabilities and the kind of consideration that can help.

Visual Impairment

Visual impairment is among the most common of disabilities. The causes are various - cataracts, glaucoma, macular degeneration, diabetic retinopathy, MS, etc. Different eye defects present different problems.

In some ways, blindness is the easiest disability for others to imagine: we all have some experience of feeling our way round blindfold or in the dark. But it is not that simple. Very few blind people see nothing at all. Some can distinguish light - but nothing else. Some have no central vision, others no side vision. Some see everything as a vague blur, others see a patchwork of blanks and defined areas. Some can see enough to read, but not to cross the road. Some perceive objects they need to negotiate but cannot recognize faces. Some see everything distorted, or doubled. If the two eyes do not work together, people may see but find it difficult to judge distance. It is not easy for sighted people to imagine all these effects. The Royal National Institute of Blind People can help with understanding some of these problems (helpline@rnib.org.uk).

Many people have some sight defect and, indeed, most experience sight changes in mid life. Provision for those with more severe problems is often also helpful to those with lesser problems. For example, someone using variable focus glasses may see well straight ahead but when looking down, through the close-up part of the lens, may easily miss a single small step unless defined by a contrasting line.

Sight is important for getting around and for gaining information, but it also plays a major role in social relationships. We see a friend across the road and wave, we smile across a room, we learn about people's reactions and emotions from their facial expressions and gestures. Those who cannot see miss much of this friendly contact. All this is relevant in church life. So greet blind people by name, touch them on the shoulder and say who you are. Introduce them to others. Say 'goodbye' when you leave them: they do not like talking into thin air!

Aids for those with impaired vision

The two most distinctive mobility aids are the white stick and the guide dog. A few use sonic and laser sticks which warn of obstacles. These aids also alert others to the needs of those who are blind.

Guide dogs in harness are working - so do not pet them and distract them from their job. The owner may well be happy to talk about the dog - but do not talk to the dog first!

Reading aids

A variety of magnifiers are available, hand-held, on stands and illuminated. Large print, Braille and Moon books may be used, according to need. There are talking books, and audio newspapers and magazines. Electronic readers can translate print into Braille or speech. Computers can enlarge print on screen, with a choice of light or dark background.

Braille is a tactile alphabet of embossed characters using different combinations of six dots to form the letters. There are lots of rules and contractions. Using Braille well takes skill and practice.

Moon is another tactile alphabet using shapes that reflect the written alphabet. It suits some people better, especially those losing sight in later life, but there is less material available in it than in Braille.

How churches can help the visually impaired

Steps and obstacles

All steps, both outside and indoors, should be marked with a white or yellow strip, periodically renewed. Single steps, especially shallow ones, quite often found at doorways, are particularly easy to miss. Watch out for lights and reflective surfaces that may dazzle those with poor sight. Try to ensure there are no obstructions and no uneven floors to trip the unwary, and avoid placing free-standing displays, that may be easily knocked over, close to entrances or main thoroughfares.

Lighting

Everybody works better in good light. Many people will find it easier to read the small print of Bibles easier in good light - but not all church buildings are well lit. For close work, people with impaired vision will need more direct light, ideally from an adjustable lamp angled so that the light falls on the reading matter from behind the reader.

  Good colour contrasts help. Most people find it easier to see dark objects on a light background (fashions in design can be quite unkind in this respect). But some are troubled by the glare of very bright white paper. Some find black on light yellow gives the best contrast. Those with poor colour vision may not notice things printed in some colours at all - this can be unfortunate where the colour change was intended to make certain information stand out!

Bibles and hymn-books

Make available some large-print Bibles and hymn books or song sheets. Even when material is on screen, some will find it difficult to see at a distance.

No longer being able to read the Bible in private devotions is a sore loss and those whose sight and mobility is failing may not find it easy to discover what is available in large-print. One tiny old lady acquired a large-print Bible but found it very heavy to handle. She was thrilled when a church friend found her the New Testament and Psalms bound together in a less cumbersome, large-print volume.

Bibles and some hymn books are available in Braille. These are bulky and expensive but they enable people to join in more fully. To buy these in case they are needed may be an unrealistic counsel of perfection, but a church should consider this seriously if there is a Braille reader in the congregation. The wide range of compilations and of new songs available today makes it harder, but not impossible, to be appropriately equipped. Brailling machines are available and with help some blind people build up their own collection of the songs most used in their churches.

It helps if the worship leader always announces clearly the first line of the song: otherwise those who cannot see are left relying on memory when they hear the tune. Some visually impaired people like help to ensure they stand up and sit down at the right times, and to find Bible readings and hymns. Others may not want this. Ask what is preferred and respect that.

Other material

Have large-print information available at the church entrance. News sheets, Bible readings and sermon notes can be taken home to read in better light and with magnification. Church magazines and lists of forthcoming activities could be made available in audio form, as well as recorded services. Modern equipment makes such provision easy, provided somebody takes on the responsibility.

The Baptist Men's Movement produces a monthly audio magazine, *Baptist Voice*, with articles from the *Baptist Times* and *BMS World Mission*. This service is provided free to people who are blind or partially sighted by Tapes for the Blind, based at Abingdon Baptist Church, 35 Ock Street, Abingdon OX14 5AG, Tel: 01235 530080.

Projection on screen

Displaying material on a single large screen, whether by overhead projector or power point, does not work for people who cannot see the screen. Large-print copies of the words in their own hands can enable some to join fully in the service.

When the first wave of new worship songs were coming into the church an older worshipper told me sadly, 'I like them, but I cannot see the screen and it's not easy to distinguish the words being sung so I take ages to learn them. Meanwhile people think I am an old fogey who's not prepared to join in anything new.' She found that it helped to buy recorded collections of songs that she could listen to at home to help the learning process.

Refreshments

When offering tea or coffee to someone with poor sight, do not fill cups too full as balancing is harder when one cannot see. Tell people what is in sandwiches, describe the choice of cakes.

Guiding someone who cannot see

Walk slightly in front, letting the blind person hold your arm. Watch out for obstacles. If you need to walk in single file, where space is restricted, say so and also indicate by bringing your guiding arm behind you.

Stop when you reach steps or stairs. Tell the blind person whether they go up or down and how many there are. When you reach the top or bottom, say so. If there is a hand-rail, put the blind person's hand on it.

When coming to a seat, let the blind person slide a hand down your arm till it rests on the back of the chair. From there, most can manage alone.

Fellowship

Elderly people who have visual impairments have been described as 'meetings people' because they have a lot of time on their hands and can be lonely, so many go from one church to another to enjoy meetings and the tea and conversation that follows. Unable to drive, they find it easier to go to day-time meetings, but offers of regular transport can make both day and evening meetings more accessible.

Conversation

When talking to someone who is visually impaired, sighted people need to be careful not to say 'Look at that', and if they see something that makes them chuckle they will need to describe what is amusing them.

When a blind person has previously known what it is to see, it is not too difficult to describe things to them. People blind from birth have never seen size, shape and colour. To envisage things, they need to build a 'picture dictionary' - 'seeing' through other people's eyes. Think about how you might describe things like the colour red, a spider's web, a plane taking off, a large oak tree, a rain cloud partially covering the sun.

Blind people often use hearing keenly, but that can have its limitations. I remember my father's distress when he could not distinguish my maturing voice from my mother's. It mattered to him to know before he spoke whether it was his wife or teenage daughter who had entered the room. We learned to say quickly something that would make it clear who was there.

Hearing Impairment

We all know people who are hard of hearing. It is one of the most common of disabilities. In my church recently I knew one person in ten had significant hearing problems - though most members would not be aware there were so many. It is very common, especially as people get older, and can be a particular problem in a social setting where lots of conversations are going on at once. People who cope quite well chatting with one or two friends in a quiet room at home may have real difficulty in a crowded hall - so they may drop out of activities they have previously enjoyed. Then they feel even more isolated.

When people are deaf it can be difficult to have a conversation with them. It is so easy just to smile, say 'Good morning', and move on. Think what it is like for them, lonely even in the midst of friends.

Joyce Costie has asked people to speak loudly - only to be told they will then get sore throats! A nurse explained that she needed to conserve her voice to talk to other patients on the ward. Other people try to speak up but soon forget and let their voices drop again.

Eventually many deaf people give up asking for this apparently simple effort of consideration.

Many people's hearing deteriorates with age, but some are deaf all their lives. In the past many profoundly deaf people attended special churches, but now more prefer to be integrated into hearing churches. That requires signers and a willingness to learn sign language on the part of hearing members.

Lip reading

Many deaf people learn to lip-read, but that requires the co-operation of speakers. Lip-readers need a clear view of the face at all times. They have difficulty if the speaker turns from side to side, or if the speaker's face is in shadow as when standing in front of a sunny window. It is easier to read the lips of those who speak clearly, with distinct lip movements, than of those who mumble and or gabble, merging sounds together. Beards and moustaches need not be a problem, provided the lips are clearly visible. One bearded minister remembers being told by a deaf lady that, as he shaved around his lips, she could read him easily.

Hearing Aids

These are a wonderful help to many people. The big problem has been that, lacking the sensitivity of the human ear, they magnify everything, not screening out irrelevant background noise as does the healthy human ear. Happily the newer electronic aids can be adjusted more finely and make it easier for those using them to hear one conversation among many.

Given a good hearing aid and an induction loop, church services may not present much problem. If the preacher speaks clearly and uses the microphones well, and holds people's attention so that there is not much coughing and shuffling, the sermon should come over quite well. Even with a hearing aid, not every sound is clearly distinguished and the deaf person often has to unscramble what they hear. This is not too difficult if the speaker has a measured delivery but is harder if speech is rapid, with words running together. Public speaking is usually better paced than conversation, which gives those who do not catch every sound more time to unscramble the words.

Move to the church hall for coffee and it may be a different matter. The buzz of many conversations, the chink of coffee cups, the crying baby, the patter of children's feet - if the hearing aid magnifies them all, it is deafening, confusing and exhausting. It is easier to go home and hope a friend will visit for a peaceful chat.

Hearing aids occasionally pick up interference from other electrical equipment. If that happens, it is the other equipment that is at fault and needs to be fixed. Joyce Costie mentions, for example, a problem she had that was caused by one of the electric guitars used at her church. Most people will not hear the problem so may dismiss it lightly, although it is a serious nuisance to the person using a hearing aid.

It can be helpful to get people new to speaking or reading scripture in a particular church to try out the amplifying equipment in advance, so that the operator can find the best setting for that voice. A little practice can also help to improve the speed and iron out other impediments to clarity. For example, some people start well but speed up or drop their voice at the end of sentences. Alerting them to such a tendency can be enough to make hearing significantly easier - for those with good hearing as well as those who need assistance!

Induction loops

Many churches have an induction loop, which is a wire connecting to the Public Address (PA) system and running round the room. Modern hearing aids have a switch (usually marked with a T) which enables them to pick up the sounds from the loop.

In theory reception should be good anywhere within the loop, though those responsible may find it works better in some parts of the room than in others (ask a deaf friend to help). One can also buy a 'tester' to enable a hearing person to check the system.

Churches that have a modern loop system may like to show the ear symbol for this on their noticeboard and on introductory hand-outs, which may also indicate where reception is found to be best.

Ideally there should be a loop in the main worship space and also in any other halls or rooms where people are likely to be speaking 'up front'. There can, however, be interference problems between loops in rooms vertically above or below one another. Horizontal proximity should not present problems.

One alternative to an induction loop has a very short-range radio transmitter attached to the PA system. Those who need it are given a tiny receiver which connects to their hearing aid. This should not interfere with rooms above or below.

A variant arrangement uses an infra-red link between the transmitter and the user. This system, sometimes used in theatres, avoids the possibility of external interference but it is essential to maintain a clear line of sight between the transmitter and user.

The Royal National Institute for the Deaf (RNID) provides helpful information on the systems available and will supply equipment.

The performance of all amplifying equipment needs to be monitored regularly. It also needs to be used properly: those with poor hearing find it frustrating when people do not speak up clearly, or refuse the microphone, or use a static microphone but move around a lot so that the signal keeps fading as they face one side and then the other. Some speakers boast they do not need amplification, which may be true for most of the audience, but if they spurn the microphone the loop system does not work and hearing aids are useless. It is not always the speaker's faulty - going to speak at a church with my throat croaky from a cold, I was dismayed to hear the stewards agreeing not to get out the microphones, as it was 'too much bother' to find the key.

Church meetings can be particularly difficult for those who are hard of hearing. To take part, one needs to hear both what is said by the officers, who usually speak from the front, and also the contributions from other members. People who are deaf may be careful to sit where they can see and hope to hear the minister and church officers, but contributions from the floor are often lost on them. Where amplification is in use, it is good to pass a roving microphone around or ask people to come forward to use the microphone at the front. For those who have always taken church membership seriously, it is hard to attend yet feel left out of any discussion.

A deaf person at church

Grace Carter, a lifelong Baptist whose hearing deteriorated from mid life on, described how it affected her church life.

> It is some fifteen years now since I first became aware of partial deafness and also the condition known as tinnitus, in my case a high-pitched shriek in both ears. Many deaf

and partially deaf people suffer from this condition and it is something one just has to learn to live with as there is no cure. I do use a hearing aid and in some circumstances this is useful, but there are many situations in which I find it to be an embarrassment.

Being a widow and leading a fairly quiet life I guess suits me, but I do attend a live Baptist Church and it is in mixing with people that life becomes harder. I love to hear a good sermon and if the speaker has a good clear voice then all is well and I can enjoy it, but if speech is very fast or there is an unusual brogue it becomes extremely difficult. I miss so much in the way of humour, for instance, as a person generally seems to drop the voice if there is something funny to be said. The congregation will laugh but I have no idea what they are laughing at and therefore feel on the outside of things.

One of the biggest problems is after the service when everyone is chatting to each other. The noise and confusion is quite hopeless and using the hearing aid makes it impossible for me to have a conversation as it just amplifies *all* the noises and I cannot even hear the person standing next to me.

I guess over the years I have tended to become more and more silent myself because of the difficulties, although I do try to join in with various activities and like to be at the church meetings, home Bible studies, etc. I help a little at the Mothers & Toddlers group in taking the register and money and entering new people, but here again noise is the problem... I have devised my own method of coping (and a smile goes a long way to help) but it is a strain and can be embarrassing.

One of the hardest things in church life is not always knowing what is going on because one has not heard and therefore not really feeling part of it. Also it is so easy to make a mistake and get things wrong. I have come off various committees through the years because I am so conscious of not getting things right through not hearing properly. I am far from being really deaf because a one-to-one conversation is good and therefore I really like my friends one at a time.

I'm so grateful that I can still hear and enjoy music. My heart goes out to people who cannot hear at all, for deafness is not really understood by hearing people.

Deaf-Blindness

This double disability often also leaves the person also unable to speak. It is hard to imagine the isolation, loneliness and frustration experienced by the deaf-blind. They experience extreme difficulties in every area of life and require special methods of communication and special help. Deaf-blind people use a distinguishing red-and-white stick.

There is a deaf-blind manual language and, for those who have become disabled later in life and were previously familiar with the written language, anyone can use the block alphabet language, spelling out a word in block capitals on the person's hand. This is slow and laborious but it can be a means of contact with someone who really needs a friend.

Impaired Mobility

There are a variety of causes of reduced mobility, including malformed limbs, cerebral palsy, polio, injury, amputation, multiple sclerosis, Parkinson's disease, and stroke. Levels of restriction range from those confined to bed or wheelchairs all the time through those who can walk a little but need a wheelchair or motorized scooter to go far, to those on crutches, and those needing a stick or just good hand-holds when getting up from seats or at steps. Some may have sound legs but problems of balance. Once again, every disabled person is different and there is no substitute for getting to know each as an individual. Here one can only alert readers to the range of possibilities.

Accessible buildings

How easy is it to enter your church and its ancillary halls? Is there a steep flight of steps, daunting to anyone not in the prime of life? Even one or two steps, which most people hardly notice, present a considerable barrier to anyone in a wheelchair - and to some with lesser mobility problems. Even if willing helpers are to hand, it is not much fun being bumped up and down such obstacles.

Since the first edition of this book, new laws have required churches, along with other public buildings, to address access for those with disabilities, so more churches are aware of the requirements - and cost - of good provision, and many have made appropriate modifications.

Ideally, there should be access by a permanent ramp running at a gentle angle, not steeper than 1 in 12. Sometimes this may be more realistically achieved at a side entrance than at the main door -

but then care should be taken to ensure this does not feel a 'second-class' way in.

For every wheelchair user there will be a number of people who can walk but with some difficulty. Some may prefer a ramp to steps, although others find ramps more demanding, especially when icy or slippery with wet leaves. Many will appreciate hand-rails and grab-handles at strategic points.

Inside the buildings there may be more steps to consider, especially if the site is not level, as well as stairs to other floors. Ideally, there should be lifts between floors, but adding these to older buildings may be prohibitively expensive. Even where a lift is provided, space may limit the size. One remodelled church won awards for good access - yet a member lamented that the lift fitted in the old tower only took five people or one wheelchair and was 'a pain' when moving a group of disabled people. Where there is no room for a lift, it may be possible to fit a stair lift for a wheelchair with a folding seat for those who can walk but not climb stairs.

Those who use crutches or sticks often cannot find anywhere convenient to stow them when they are sitting down. On the floor they may present a hazard, tripping other people up, and be difficult for their owners to retrieve. Clips to anchor sticks to tables are available, though not often seen. A church might usefully acquire some.

Pews do not lend themselves to easy accommodation of wheelchairs, which can be a potentially dangerous obstruction in the aisles. Some people with disabilities find pews almost impossible to sit on. The chairs that have replaced them in many churches may not be much better. It is easier to move them to allow a wheelchair user to sit with family or friends, but some people with limited mobility will be more comfortable and more independent if there are some chairs with firm arms to help them get up and down. Fixed pews at least offer the one in front to pull on, or as a firm support while standing. If the church retains pews but wants to make some wheelchair spaces, it is better not to do this right at the front, which is too conspicuous, or at the back, where visibility will be limited, especially when the congregation stands.

In church halls and meeting rooms too, there should be some chairs with good arms and relatively high seats. Low chairs without arms require a certain agility and are difficult for many older people.

How accessible is the platform? High pulpits are used less today and more members of the congregation take part in leading worship. In many churches the old rails around communion tables have been removed, and wide low platforms with two or three steps are popular. Often there is no support to help those who may be unsteady on steps. Some deacons find it quite difficult to carry a communion tray down two or three steps with nothing to hold on to.

One worshipper with an artificial leg says she can mount her church's platform with cheerful inelegance on her own on a Saturday to do the flowers, but she is less happy to do this 'her way' conspicuously on a Sunday to read the lesson. She has to ensure there will be someone at hand to steady her. Uncluttered modern design may look good but feel unsafe.

Access to toilets is also important. This should be free of steps. There should be at least one spacious disabled toilet with strategically sited grab-rails. There should be a washbasin in the cubicle, with taps that are easy to push on and off.

Wheelchair users

Modern access requirements mean that more public buildings, churches included, now have ramps and lifts and other features to make it easier for those using wheelchairs or motorized scooters. But the difficulties for wheelchair users do not only lie in physical access. Their heads are on a lower level than most adults so they can all too easily be overlooked - literally and metaphorically. Even when people talk to them, they continually have to look upwards which is not comfortable. They appreciate friends who sit or kneel to talk eye to eye.

Some wheelchairs are power-driven, which increases the user's independence. People with very limited arm movement can manage these. The disadvantage is the weight of the electric batteries. Some users revert to the manual chair when going to buildings where there is no alternative to stairs, because if friends need to lift them, the powered chair is just too heavy.

Make full use of good premises

If you have made good provision, indicate this with the wheelchair sign on the church noticeboard. Advertise the provision for those with disabilities in the local press, community centres and Social Service offices. The church that has gone to the trouble and expense of ensuring good access may reasonably draw attention to this in outreach!

Well-equipped premises may be made available for other meetings during the week. An accessible church hall, for example, at Christ Church, Stantonbury Campus, Milton Keynes, became the weekly venue for the Spinning Wheels, a wheelchair dance group, providing a time of recreation and fellowship. Welcoming such groups on church premises also gives an opportunity for friendly contact with church people.

Conversation with these dancers revealed that, while the carefully planned 'new town' was generally good in provision for citizens with impaired mobility, even there transport was a problem. The special bus service was oversubscribed and did not extend to evenings. Taxis were reluctant to take wheelchair users, who take more time to get in and out. Churches need to be aware of such matters, because reliable, regular and cheerful transport provision can make all the difference when it comes to attending worship or other meetings.

Disabilities of Hands and Arms

These may be less immediately obvious yet are possibly even more restricting than leg defects. They include those without full use of an arm, as well as those without an arm at all, those whose cerebral palsy leaves little control over arms and hands, those twisted and weakened by arthritis, and those who 'just' have a tremor that interferes with fine finger control.

It is possible for someone to be quite strong and able to lift a large and heavy pan yet be unable to hold a tiny communion cup. This may well be more a matter of balance than grip. An understanding friend alongside can take the glass from the tray and pour the communion wine into a larger cup. One mother virtually forgot this as a problem until her daughters both left home and in mid-service she found herself without quiet assistance. Whatever is appropriate should be done with the minimum of embarrassing fuss.

Sharing a communal meal, especially a stand-up buffet, can be embarrassing and people may miss out for fear of fuss. Again it helps if problems are discussed with friends in advance, so that they are alert to help appropriately and unobtrusively. It may mean carrying the filled plate to a table - and then not leaving the person to sit alone in a corner while others mill around with plates in hand. It may mean serving food to save clumsy reaching, half filling cups (and being alert to replenish them) to reduce spills, or cutting food to manageable size. Some people find it better to cradle a cup in two hands, rather than shaking it from the handle; others may bring a special cup, perhaps lidded against spills. All those with cerebral palsy will have difficulty in carrying liquids.

> It is impossible for us to move, or for many of us even to stand, holding a cup, glass, or jug with liquid in it. So we develop strategies to cope. Take the kettle to the mug, take the lemonade to the garden in the bottle ... When I walk into a room where I know I am going to be offered something to drink, I make sure I choose a seat near a piece of furniture that can serve as a table ... If I am among a crowd of strangers, however hospitable, I often find it better to refuse anything to drink, as do other CP sufferers I know. Why should this be necessary? Most people are only too willing to accommodate me, but inevitably there is some fuss over rearranging chairs or finding a suitable table, and I become the focus of attention, which embarrasses me and makes me nervous and therefore more likely to spill the drink and then everyone else gets embarrassed. It's all too much trouble.

The conduct of worship

This can have a lot of pitfalls for someone with limb disability. Working out carefully in advance with colleagues where and when physical assistance may be required will avoid a lot of misunderstanding, enable them to appreciate the difficulties faced, and ensure a minimum of distraction for the congregation.

Arthritis

This painful and disabling condition is all too common. It can affect various parts of the body and friends need to be guided by individual sufferers on what helps them. Often it restricts mobility and the use of arms and hands. Although prevalent among older people, arthritis is not confined to them. The next contributor was still quite young when, after some previous problems, she became completely housebound for a time:

> Months of inactivity, pain and sleeplessness followed. I was glad of the practical help given in the home by family, friends and folk of the church family. I was diagnosed as having Cervical Spondylitis and arthritis of the spine, and had to wear a cervical collar.
>
> During the time I was housebound I appreciated the services on the radio and TV and was amazed to discover how other Christians who are housebound do not realize and avail themselves of these opportunities for worship.
>
> On my return to worship at church I was unable to sit in the pew. So I took along my own chair. There was nowhere inconspicuous to put it and more often than not it was in the aisle, where folk kept bumping me, or at the front where the folk I was with couldn't even sit with me. I soon made myself cushions to fit the pews and now I have cushions, will travel! The thrill of being able to attend worship when you are disabled should never be underestimated.
>
> Our church caretaker always made certain that my chair, one of a number of soft stacking chairs the church had, was at the right place for meetings, and got quite indignant when others sat on it.

Transport to and from church is vital for those who have little mobility and, for those with neck and arm problems, help with carrying bags and books.

From an arthritic's point of view, the warm strong handshake, the thump on the back, the bear hug can all mean days of added pain.

I came to terms with my situation but others kept asking why I wasn't back as I had always been. On the other hand, because I now wore a collar, many thought I had lost my marbles as well and talked to me via my husband - the 'Does he take sugar?' syndrome.

It is difficult as a woman to be unable to carry trays, stand and prepare food, wash and wipe up. All the things people still presume the women in our church will do! Buffet meals at church are a nightmare when you are unable to carry your own food or stand around and eat it. This is a real problem for elderly folk as well and there are seldom enough chairs for all to sit down. It may be better for people to remain in their seats and have the food brought to them.

It is much easier to talk to people if they come down to your level, but if you just have to sit and are unable to circulate you are often very isolated, as folk just leave you there. You have plenty of time to talk to them if they would only come to you.

Many physically disabled people have a lot of time to sit and think and have a lot to contribute if helped to do so.

Leading worship is not a problem if the platform is easily accessible, there is a reading desk for books and notes, and occasional help is at hand.

Spinal Damage

This brings us to backache, a common problem in sedentary Western society. Many people experience it at some time and it tends to recur. For some, damage is severe and prolonged. Both standing and sitting for long may be difficult. The most comfortable rest position will depend on the part of the back affected. Some need to lie flat, others to recline slightly propped, others to sit upright with good support. The church seating may not lend itself to such positions, but where there is the will there is usually a way round this.

After spinal surgery, my mother longed to return to church for Easter morning. She could walk a little but not sit up. We tipped the car seat right back and loaded a folding mattress and cushions. She had planned where she could recline unobstrusively, and how we must arrive in good time and sneak in round the back so that the elaborate preparations would pass unnoticed. She had not reckoned on her young grandson who leapt out, seized the foam mattress and cushions and marched in the front door, announcing, 'This is grandmother's bed!' Her dismay soon vanished in the warmth of her friends' welcome - and they were made aware of what it took to attend.

A young woman with a neck injury that has also led to lower back problems writes:

> I have tried to carry on as much as normal and not let it interfere in life, but it has been difficult and many activities have either been curtailed or stopped altogether. I have good days and bad days. The good days I feel great and happy, with only the occasional twinge which causes me a jolt back to reality - that maybe I'm overdoing it and I need to be careful. The bad days are really bad and I could cry

with the pain and I need painkillers to help free me so that I can do basic activities, such as bathing or sitting. That really gets me depressed ... I try to carry on as normal and do things I used to do before the accident but I know that at times it's impossible. My faith is strengthened by problems I've encountered in ways I can hardly explain. I thought I had patience but it's increased now.

In services I tend to sit at the back so if I do get discomfort and pain I can at least stand up without causing distraction to others in the congregation, or at times I need to sit down and I find this quite embarrassing as I feel people watching.

Heart and Chest Problems

These are common, especially as people get older. The advice below came from a minister with experience of emphysema, bronchiectisis and a series of heart attacks.

Buildings and rooms should be kept at moderate temperatures. Overheating can be as much a problem as underheating - although the latter is more likely to be the problem at church. Warmth is a common need, e.g. for people with arthritis or poor circulation.

Buildings with lots of steps can be exhausting. Ramps may help those in wheelchairs but they are no solution for those with heart conditions, who find them as bad as stairs.

In much modern worship we expect people to stand for long periods, singing worship songs, and this can be exhausting. One can always sit down - but then you cannot see anything, especially the overhead projection screen, and you probably feel self-conscious and less part of things.

People with chest problems may not be able to come out on cold winter evenings; also they have to be conscious of the greater risk of infections in crowded rooms. So people who may be able to be very active in summer months may suddenly become 'unreliable' and almost reclusive. They might, however, be able to hold a regular house group in their home, or appreciate an occasional house communion (perhaps at Christmas or Easter). They might even invite neighbours and would appreciate being able to participate in the church's mission.

If it is the minister who has these problems, the church could enquire whether it might be helpful to hold deacons' meetings or any small committees at the manse rather than on the church premises.

There can be a real ministry in enabling people with heart problems to meet together on an informal level for mutual support and encouragement.

Speech Defects

Human society is verbal and anything that interferes with communication is hard for those affected. Speech disabilities range from a slight but embarrassing stammer to complete lack of spoken language. They are often associated with other conditions - like deafness or cerebral palsy. Others suffer speech loss as a result of accident, stroke or disease. Whatever the cause, to know what you want to say and yet be incapable of getting it out must be terribly frustrating.

False assumptions make it worse. Because speech problems are very common in people with severe learning disabilities, anyone having serious difficulty with speech is often wrongly assumed to have little understanding. Similarly, slurred speech may be assumed to stem from drunkenness, and anyone reduced to communicating by desperate gestures risks being thought violent.

Misunderstanding creates its own barriers. People become confused and frightened when they cannot make themselves understood, so they avoid any direct approach, and this increases their feeling of rejection. Meanwhile, other people are afraid to get involved with these 'alarming' folk, because they do not understand what it is like to be isolated by such disability.

Happily, for some at least, the ease of modern word-processing is opening up new ways of communication, revealing articulate minds through the written word.

Those who have speech but wrestle with stammers and stutters usually find that nervousness aggravates their difficulty - and they are not much helped by friends who get impatient or who 'kindly' supply the word they are trying to get out. Understanding friends may counteract the loss of self-confidence caused by these problems, and sometimes that contributes to overcoming the stammer.

Dietary Restrictions

A number of conditions are controlled by diet. Nowadays, when many people opt for special diets (low fat, vegetarian, etc.) for reasons of general health consciousness or ecological principle, it may seem easier to ask for something different. Even so, many who *must* take special care are embarrassed to say, 'Sorry, I can't have that', and some sadly find it easier to opt out of social gatherings altogether.

Some churches arrange communal meals and members also entertain at home. Whenever refreshments are served, make sure plain water is readily available, both hot and cold, so that no-one has to 'make a fuss' asking for it. Some savoury biscuits alongside the chocolate ones may help John who has diabetes to feel more included - but what about Mary who cannot digest the gluten in the wheat biscuits? People on special diets get used to declining, but appreciate it when something they *can* have is quietly on offer. Then they will not feel peculiar.

Even a small piece of communion bread can have too much gluten for a person with coeliac disease, although the wafers used in other churches are 'safe'. A piece of rice cake or gluten-free bread can be substituted - but be sensitive about the 'one loaf of which we all partake' (1 Corinthians 10.17)! Make sure people know this is available.

Asthma and Other Allergies

Many people suffer from allergic conditions and the substances which cause their reactions are numerous. The reactions can vary from a mild, itchy rash to a sudden, life-threatening attack called anaphylaxis, which involves swelling and obstruction of the airways and possible death within minutes if medical help is not received. Often those at risk will carry an antidote.

Allergy-causing agents are often food-stuffs, the most common being eggs, milk, nuts, strawberries and shellfish, although it could be absolutely anything. When someone needs to avoid one ingredient, like orange juice or sunflower oil, they quickly discover that, apart from the obvious appearances, these may crop up in a wide range of prepared foods. For those who are allergic to several possible ingredients avoiding them, except with food prepared at home, can be quite difficult.

Allergic reactions tend to get worse with repeated exposure: the baby whose allergy first appeared in a swollen cheek where her father kissed her after nibbling peanuts became the young woman fighting for life after similarly accidental exposure to lettuce served with a spoon which had touched a salad containing nuts.

For anyone with a severe allergic condition there are obvious implications in church fellowships where meals are often shared. It is important to be sensitive when someone asks to know the ingredients of a particular dish, and to be diligent in discovering exactly what has gone into its preparation. A simple 'I'm sure it's all right' will not be sufficient and may result in the person being embarrassed and perhaps withdrawing from such social occasions. It may be helpful for people with allergies to be invited to serve themselves first at large communal meals, before spoons get mixed up and nuts are accidentally dropped into salads.

It is not just foods. Dust is a threat to many asthmatics. Even when everything has been made new, all are not safe: the fumes from new paints and adhesives may present a threat to those with chemical allergies. Modern buildings are less draughty than in the past, but they can be too well sealed against fresh air and then fumes can take months to disperse completely. A few people can effectively be excluded from the church by such problems, which must be particularly frustrating when they have been involved in the planning and fund-raising for the improvements!

Diabetes

People with diabetes live with it all the time. They become the experts - but they need co-operation from others and can do with someone who will keep an eye on them without making a fuss. This might mean not letting a weary minister 'doze', as one explains:

Fast asleep in a deacons' meeting - not unusual, you might think, but I was the Chairman! It has happened twice to me. But it was not 'sleep', it was a 'hypo', known to all Insulin Dependent Diabetics (IDDs) but largely not understood by others. A 'hypo' is a hypoglycaemic (under-sugared) reaction to insulin. 'But you can't take sugar, can you?' Yes, I can and I need it. The secret of successful diabetic control is 'balance' between insulin and carbohydrate (sugar/starch).

On another occasion I felt the early symptoms in the hymn before I was to preach. I slipped in some sugar lumps but could not continue doing that once I started preaching. After ten minutes I could not think what the next word ought to be, nor could I recall what I had just said. Stubbornly I forged ahead (stubbornness often accompanies a hypo), not really knowing what I was saying. I was glad to announce the closing hymn, give the blessing and retreat, unusually for me, to the vestry. After a while my wife turned in. 'What's wrong?' she asked, not having noticed anything - and nor had anyone else! It was comforting to realize something must have held together (the alternative is unthinkable!).

Thirty-two years after diagnosis and something over 23,000 injections later, I am remarkably well and thankful for careful clinical care and wise GPs.

Once someone has diabetes, they have it for life. It is not visible but it always has to be reckoned with. It is serious, and some of the long-term complications can be life-threatening. They include blindness, kidney failure, heart disease, damage to nerve endings and blood vessels. Good diabetic control gives the person the best chance of avoiding these complications, though this is not guaranteed.

Control involves a balance between diet, activity and medication to keep the glucose level right. For some (often those diagnosed later in life) careful diet suffices. Others need tablets too. IDDs have to inject insulin in addition to careful diet. For anyone newly diagnosed, there is a lot to learn and it must be learned quickly.

When a child has diabetes it is not easy to allow enough freedom while making sure all the *extra* boundaries are kept. Those leading children's and youth work need to talk to parents and learn enough about the condition to do and say the right thing. If the young people's group is going away together, the youth leader, primary carer and young person with diabetes should plan together how to manage the diabetes while out of routine. Close supervision will chafe. A small peer group, aware of what might crop up and how to deal with it, can be a great asset, and is often readily recruited.

People often recognize the signs of a hypo themselves and take preventive action, eating something sugary. If your neighbour in church takes out a Mars Bar in the middle of the sermon, don't look disapproving. Do not expect a share either - it will all be needed!

If someone does not notice they are going hypo, the signs may become obvious to others. Speech may become slurred, walking unsteady. This can be mistaken for drunkenness. The person may become cold and sweaty, which can look like a heart problem. They may become very difficult and even aggressive. If you know they have diabetes, always consider the possibility of a hypo. Things may not be making any sense to the person affected and short-term retention may be lacking. Reasoning will be a waste of time. Do not argue but be firmly persuasive: 'You're going hypo. Eat this *now*' - and make them. This may not come easily but, if they have reached that state, they need it. Give them biscuits, chocolate, sweets - they may resist, knowing it is not normally 'allowed', but do not give in.

If unconsciousness happens, get medical help. The person cannot swallow safely and should not be given food or drink.

After a hypo, do not expect instant recovery. A person needs time to get back to normal and may feel very tired. He or she may become unusually dependent, which can be embarrassing to the carer and onlookers. There may be no recollection of what has occurred.

The general dietary principles for diabetics are those of healthy eating: low fat, high fibre, unrefined. Lunch and dinner are often not too difficult; the tricky bit is 'pudding'. Fresh fruit is a good alternative. It is kind to offer something which takes a similar time to eat: instead of fruit pie, an apple or pear, instead of mousse, a banana. Diabetic diets have gained enormously from healthy-eating foods - diet yogurts, sugarfree jellies and jams, and fruit tinned in natural juice are often nicer and less expensive than 'diabetic' products. Tea, as a meal, can be rather a minefield. People with diabetes may not be geared to eating at that time of day. If they decline, do not press them.

Those who use insulin or tablets have to take timing into account. They need to balance medication and food intake: they are not just being awkward. Prolonged activity without food is unwise. When preparing 'manning' rotas, ask when they can help; the 12-2 slot may be difficult.

Events and outings need careful preparation and last-minute changes cause problems. A sudden decision to walk another half-hour before lunch can give real difficulty. So can a service in which each hymn is sung three times unexpectedly. The long celebration may be great - but not for IDDs!

A check-list on helping diabetics

- Try to ensure there is always someone 'in the know' about the IDD.
- Do not let activities last longer than two hours without a refreshment break.
- At conferences ensure that sessions do not overrun into meal times and allow time between session and meal (for injecting).
- Make sure sugar, sweets or a sweet drink are available - most IDDs carry sugar or glucose.
- Make sure there is a cloakroom easily available, where they can inject.
- Look out for symptoms of 'trouble' - aggressive or out-of-character behaviour, irrationality, sweating, a 'high'. Be ready to be firmly persuasive.
- Watch for any signs of 'trouble' as people disperse, especially from activities out of normal routine. Make sure the IDD is safe to drive. He or she may need to eat. It is both very dangerous and an offence to drive under the influence of drink or drugs, including insulin.

Hidden Disabilities

Most people seek to keep their disabilities unobtrusive, but hidden disabilities present their own problems. Many people have conditions not immediately visible to others but still restricting. One writes:

> Those with disabilities which are not obvious in the normal run of events suffer embarrassment when asked to perform tasks requiring strength, reach or endurance. 'Hidden' disability is psychologically painful when limitations are

exposed. For example, the 'normal'-looking man may be asked (even in these politically correct times) to lift or carry heavy items, assist in changing a punctured tyre ... Faced with a high luggage rack, people look round for a tall man ... When he has to decline in embarrassment, he may well be met with disbelief, scorn or even ridicule. An explanation is often fruitless.

Age can actually help here. The well-built youth who was self-conscious about opting out of heavy lifting - like moving furniture or lifting the baptistry lid - found that by later middle age plenty of men were wary of straining weak backs or taxing ailing hearts. It was much easier then to say, 'I'm sorry but I can't help with lifting'.

Unnecessary fuss is dreadful. Those leading 'a normal life' despite a disabling condition prefer to keep it hidden, not dominant. They fear possible embarrassment - even just that involved in asking for some small thing that would help. Friends aware of particular difficulties can be alert to ensure suitable provision is made quietly and discreetly.

Averting embarrassing situations often involves self-imposed restrictions, like declining to join in some activities altogether or avoiding going to new places. If we wonder why someone never joins in or seems not to take his fair share of work, the reason just might be some hidden disability.

Stoma

Colostomies and ileostomies are among the most embarrassing of disabilities - even the workings of the normal bowel are a taboo subject! Quite a lot of people, as a result of intestinal problems or disease, end up with a stoma - an opening in the abdominal wall to empty the bowel. Long-term stomas can be a drastic but life-saving remedy. Not immediately visible, these may be noticeable in other ways. After many years of resultant good health, one man reflects:

> The main problem I find in coping with a colostomy is the risk of embarrassment, especially if with people who are not aware of the problem. The colostomy can start working with little or no warning, and can be noisy and smelly. When working or about to work, there is often a 'queasy' feeling which at best makes me want to sit quietly for a few minutes and can be very tiring for a short period. Going to the lavatory to change the dressing can take a long time, and the need to do so can arise suddenly, both of which can be awkward. On a bad day the dressing can leak and clothing become soiled, adding to the problems. Diet is not a particular problem for me, although I avoid foods which produce smelly wind and anything that has a laxative effect.

The healthy colon is a very long stretch of intestine which extracts water from foodstuffs into the body. If much of it is lost, extra drinks will probably be needed to maintain right fluid balance, especially in hot weather. At the same time, the unabsorbed water will result in very moist faeces which may be messy to deal with.

One elderly lady, in hospital with a stoma after an operation for bowel cancer, confided to her minister that it would be impossible for her to go to church again, even though she had been a faithful member all her life. She explained that she would not be able to go anywhere that did not have a lavatory with its own washbasin. The communal row of washbasins in the church toilets would not offer privacy for changing dressings. Once known, her problem was easily solved. The vestry had the required facilities and, given a key, she could go there unobtrusively.

Epilepsy

Epilepsy is another, often 'hidden', condition that affects people in a wide variety of ways and degrees of severity, so it is hard to generalize. Epilepsy, a chronic neurological condition, may be evident from birth or develop later. Some people have seizures frequently, others rarely. Some have a clear warning or 'aura' before a seizure and can take precautions, but others get no prior indication. Some black out and become unconscious (a *tonic clonic seizure*, indicating the typical stiffening followed by shaking, previously known as *grand mal*). Others just look blank and clearly not 'with it', yet are just as obviously conscious (*absence*, previously *petit mal*). Many people with the condition can be well controlled by medication, enabling them to lead normal lives.

The cause of the condition and the triggers causing a seizure is often unknown. Among the possibilities are genetic factors, brain damage, serious accident, alcohol, stress, and flickering lights. This range of possibilities can in itself raise big questions for those with the condition and their families.

People who suffer from epilepsy are normal people with an illness. Unless very severe, it does not affect mental abilities or spiritual growth, though it may require care not to overdo things physically. These are people with the same reasoning abilities as anyone else, and the same need of companionship, friendship and love. Most usually feel normal and can play a full part in church life. A number of accredited Baptist ministers have epilepsy.

In an epileptic seizure there is a temporary change in the way the brain cells work. A person having a seizure stiffens and becomes rigid rather than limp, as when fainting, and is therefore more likely to be injured in falling. Seizures can frighten onlookers, as the sufferer may become blue (owing to lack of oxygen) and begin dribbling from the mouth. Incontinence in seizures is common. Some are later sick. After a seizure, headache and amnesia are common, not to mention a badly chewed tongue which will become ulcerated. Although alarming, the seizure itself is very unlikely to prove fatal, and the sick person is not going to hurt other people.

What to do during a seizure

DO
- lay the person on his or her side and undo tight clothing to help with breathing
- cushion the person's head
- stay calm and clear people away
- support any friends, relatives or bystanders who may be frightened, upset or embarrassed.

DO NOT
- try to restrain the person during a seizure (but try to soften any fall)
- put your fingers in the mouth (they may get severely damaged)
- give the person anything to drink
- leave the person alone until he or she has recovered
- be frightened.

In most cases, unless the person who has epilepsy tells them, others will never know. It is, however, sensible to tell some friends and the church leaders to make sure there are people around who know how to help without fear or fuss if the need should arise. Practically, the church might keep some spare trousers and underwear handy, like the playgroup keeps 'spares' against accidents.

Those who have epilepsy never understand the effect their blackouts have on other people unless they have seen someone else having a seizure. If they can talk openly about their condition and specific needs, their friends will be prepared and feel less helpless next time.

Epilepsy is not demonic in origin, so 'deliverance ministry' is not an appropriate response. It will harm rather than help. If the church prays for healing - which is never inappropriate - remember the whole family, as they all suffer when one member has the condition. Bear in mind that the person with epilepsy, however much helped by prayer, will still need to continue to take medication - in order to retain a driving licence, amongst other things!

When first compiling this material, I consulted Iain Collins, then a Baptist Superintendent Minister whose work included visiting many churches as guest preacher. When I saw him again some months later, he told me that our conversation had prompted him sometimes to mention from the pulpit that he had epilepsy, in a way he had not done previously. He found he never did so without someone making a point of thanking him afterwards - often a young person trying to come to terms with the condition. They were much encouraged by hearing this respected minister speak of it. He had not previously realized how such mention of his condition could help others.

Myalgic Encephalomyelitis (ME)

This condition is also known as Chronic Fatigue Syndrome (CFS) and Post-Viral Fatigue Syndrome (PVFS). The effects of ME are both variable and unpredictable - this presents problems not only to those with the condition but also to those who want to help them. A person with ME may be seen out shopping one day and yet next day be unable to go to church, or even get out of bed. From hour to hour there can be great variation. One may appear to be in blooming health - even when the muscles are about to give out - so it is helpful when friends accept that what the person says is so.

ME always involves muscle weakness and exhaustion after very little activity, but other symptoms vary. They may include muscle pain, food and chemical allergies, over-sensitivity to heat and cold, dizziness, bladder dysfuntion, mental debility. Those with the condition may find high noise levels overwhelming - in worship as well as in social activities. They will welcome a gentle approach to hand-shaking too - no vigorous back-slapping or fist-pumping, please!

The muscles fatigue very quickly. Standing is more difficult than walking, since the same muscles are in use all the time. Those conducting services should be aware when they ask people to stand for significant periods, as through a succession of songs, and might invite those who find this difficult to sit. Probably several people will be glad to, and then the one who is barely able to stand through half a chorus will feel less self-conscious about it. In some cases, even a wheelchair is not sufficient answer: some form of bed in a suitable corner might make attendance at services more possible.

Social occasions are difficult as they usually involve milling around to chat - often in church halls that are not all that comfortably appointed. A scattering of chairs is helpful, but so is understanding that absence does not mean the person with ME wants to be unsociable. Friends need to be alert to pick up distress signs - like the need for a chair. They can make sure such provision is made anyway - and they can ask without fuss what is needed just now.

People with ME also have gifts to offer. When they have in some measure come to terms with their situation, some, for example, have time to be good listeners.

Progressive Conditions

Various debilitating, progressive conditions can run for a short or long term without known cure. Those with such conditions and the carers, on whom they increasingly depend, need all the support they can get, both practical and spiritual. Multiple sclerosis (MS), for example, often lasts for many years, with its typical pattern of remissions and relapses, hopes raised and disappointed. The understanding needed here includes recognition that those affected have better and worse days and what they can do varies accordingly.

Another progressive condition is motor neurone disease. This neurodegenerative disease leads to weakness and wasting of muscles with resultant loss of mobility in limbs, and difficulties in speech, swallowing and breathing.

A daughter, herself disabled, cared for her father, long a faithful church member, over the four years to his death:

Social Services provided various helpful aids, such as a Zimmer walking frame, easyriser chair, commode. Unfortunately most of the church folk seemed afraid to visit or offer much help. The only practical help was given by my aunt ... in her eighties, and a friend of my father's who did not go to church! I think their lack of concern was partly due to ignorance about the illness. They could not and did not even try to understand his slurred speech. He found this most hurtful.

My father was mentally alert and had excellent hearing until the end of his life. When his speech failed completely, he first used to write down what he wanted to say; later on he was loaned a Communicator from the hospital ... which prints out the messages on paper tapes.

However, he was collected for the church services, but had to be carried up the stairs in a most undignified way as the church had no ramp for wheelchairs.

Life on Dialysis

Medical developments prolong lives, though sometimes with new kinds of disability. The chances of a church having a member with a transplanted organ increase. A significant number of people are now on dialysis, awaiting kidney transplants. A Baptist minister who spent six and a half years on dialysis, says the worst part is the time it takes. One might imagine that a person on dialysis would have lots of time to read, but it is not that simple: the body cells undergo dramatic changes and concentration is likely to be poor during and for a while after the session.

> Each week I spent at least 18 hours dialysing! This is a sizeable chunk out of anyone's week... Fortunately, the fact that this machine was at home allowed me to be flexible, fitting the dialysis sessions around hospital visits, deacons' meetings, Bible studies.
>
> It did not always go smoothly. Medical emergencies can be frightening. Machine failure, blood leaks, clotted needles meant either the hospital team rushing to the house or me rushing to the hospital. For my wife and daughters this was not always easy ... few understood the cost to them...

Holidays meant taking the machine with us. This involved detailed planning, two cars - one to transport the machine and medical supplies, the other for the family. But amazingly we managed ... the New Forest, Scotland, even Switzerland. It sounds good, but at times it was almost too much for us.

One of the problems is the 'sick man syndrome'. Although you prove time and again that you can cope as a kidney patient and hold down a full-time job, people still regard you as being chronically incapacitated, 'a sick man'. 80% of all kidney patients are unemployed. It is nearly impossible to get mortgages, life insurance, etc. This can be depressing, especially when all you are allowed to drink is 500ml of fluid a day and 60g of protein, and no food containing potassium, e.g. chocolate, coffee, fruit juices, vegetables and fruit... What you long for is encouragement, not pity.

Life on dialysis is not easy, but at least there is hope. For me, the transplant meant 'a new birth'. It is not the complete answer, but it transformed my life and I shall be ever grateful to the family who in the midst of their bereavement gave permission for the organ of their loved one to be used. Grateful too for the skill and dedication of the Renal Unit, and, above all, thankful to God and my family for enabling me to enjoy the new life to the full.

Although the church and Christian friends have been wonderfully supportive, some things could have made life easier and more manageable.

Awareness - very few understood what was involved: the time, the anxieties we found as a family, the stress, the vulnerability.

Insensitivity- some well-meaning Christians with their enthusiasm for healing and the supernatural can do more harm than good. There were times when, if my faith had not been strong, I would have walked out on Christianity and never returned. Thankfully, I had no such people in my church, but they were around, and at times I was tempted to walk.

Pragmatism - at times we could have done with some help in the garden! Who wouldn't!

I should like to thank all those who did walk the journey with us, who were aware of what we were going through, who prayed and supported us spiritually, and who helped us practically.

Being Neutrapenic

Sometimes the side effects of treatment create their own disabilities. The suppression of normal immune reactions by chemotherapy brings its own problems, some relevant in the church context.

During the most vulnerable periods we used to get to church during the first hymn and slip out again while the final hymn was being sung. Once I even sat upstairs ... on my own to avoid contact with potential coughs and colds. I found this rather depressing, as though my worship was only half completed. It made me realize that for me 'going to church' consists of two equally significant components, the social contact with my fellow members being just as important as being present at the service. This was much improved when friends realized that a simple cold would be likely to develop into something rather serious if I caught it. I began to sit in my usual place again and at the end of the service people used to gather around me ... They used to make a wide circle and we would shout conversation across to each other and laugh at the situation together.

One thing which did worry me was 'Had the communion cups been thoroughly washed up?' 'Who last used this cup?' This slight anxiety somewhat spoilt the joy of being able to participate in communion ... heightened even more when we were worshipping at Anglican churches with a common cup. Instead of concentrating on the service I found myself praying, 'Please, God, don't let me catch any bugs'. I know that it made my husband feel anxious too.

When she was able to venture to the church hall]

Having to be seated was very hard. Not being on a level with everyone else made it so difficult to join in conversations and as people rushed around one could easily feel overlooked. Not being able to move from place to place was an awful disadvantage too. I never experienced this sort of frustration when out in the wheelchair in the secular world. There I never met with anything other than smiles, helpfulness and a sense of inclusion. It was easier when I had remained in the church and people had formed the circle around me. I am sure that it is all a question of body space and neck angles!

Part of the Church's Life

While the conditions considered above are not a comprehensive overview, they should convey that a wide range of disabilities may be present, seen and unseen, in the local church. It is easy for people coping with such problems to feel left out and overlooked on the fringe of church life. It is, nevertheless, possible for people with severe disabilities to be well integrated and a creative force in the church, drawing out others' gifts but also contributing their own.

Baptism by immersion may present practical problems but, when there is the will, these can often be surmounted. If people fuss too much about 'how', candidates may find it easier to decide against immersion - and bear the pain of being 'different'.

For people with disabilities, who often need to receive help, it is especially precious to be able to serve. After many years in ministry, Howard Williams once observed to me that he was 'constantly amazed by the contribution to the church of people who could easily be excused any extras'.

I remember Annie, a street-wise old Cockney saint, with weak heart and little sight, who helped with the washing up at church every Sunday and helped run the tuck shop for a tough inner-city Boys' Club midweek. At the geriatric clinic she got a roomful of dismally waiting folk enjoying a jolly sing-song, with the amused approbation of the nurse in charge.

Another active church member has a weak right side and speech defect resulting from whooping cough in babyhood. Baptized at fourteen, she has served as Sunday School teacher, Girls' Brigade officer, and on her church's Pastoral Care Team. She has enjoyed helping with the church's annual 'Holiday at Home' for those unable to go away, including some with disabilities. Her advice is:

If there is a message I can give ... perhaps it is this: Do give people with disabilities a chance to lead a normal life. Give help when it is needed, but *please remember that these people want to be one of you, not set apart.*

In another church a young woman finds the limitations of a spinal injury hard: 'I used to enjoy going on the weekend retreats ... but I find this difficult now ...' People know she has a serious problem, and she values the support and encouragement they give her, but that does not stop her minding that she cannot 'pull her weight'.

I also enjoyed helping with Sunday lunches at church, but when my back problem flared up again I had to let them down, which caused me much distress as I felt a failure, although everyone was very kind and understanding. When I do help with lunches, I try and do most that's asked of me, but I do have problems lifting ... [and] I'm embarrassed to say I can't do it.

There is a delicate balance in this. As another writes:

The disabled person has to beware of disabling their self-esteem by believing certain tasks are beyond them when with some application the over-facing problem can be tackled successfully. Other people have to have the sensitivity on the one hand to be aware of and anticipate the disabled person's limitation, and on the other to know when and how to encourage them to achieve a task ... The key consideration for the church is to exercise a vigorous policy of *inclusiveness* in its attitude toward the disabled, rather than the exclusiveness which has prevailed in the past. An illustration of this is that a member with cerebral palsy has recently produced our church Christmas card. His disability means he has no use of his arms and hands; his ability meant that he produced the cover design, lay-out and inside text by computer - all done with two toes on his left foot!

Sport is another important communal activity, and especially important among young people; what is possible will vary, but do not assume that disability rules people out automatically. If one sport is out, there is likely to be another which is possible. Sports and games which rely on precision and skill rather than strength can boost confidence. Some will enjoy bowls, ten-pin bowling, snooker, billiards, or table-tennis. Outdoor sports like sailing, riding, karting, and even motor sports are within the ability of many with disabilities. One of the champion swimmers in my school had a leg wasted by polio; she was a bit lopsided for style events but few could match her speed.

The message is really not to keep staring at the door that is closed but to look for an alternative route. Disabilities are real and restricting but a bit of creative thinking can often overcome obstacles or find other opportunities.

Healing - the vexed issue

Many contributors have mentioned problems over the way healing ministry is often understood - or mis-understood. One minister, physically disabled from birth, explained:

> A problem that often arises in the church is that people who are very committed to the healing ministry see the disabled as ripe for it. They can often cause spiritual depression by their insistence on laying on of hands when it is the disabled person who has taken his condition to the Lord, asking for the ability to cope with and triumph over his limitations, *and learned to live with them.* That is the realistic experience of healing.

Another minister had no crisis of faith as a result of prolonged suffering, but felt vulnerable in relation to healing ministry: 'Handled with an inadequate theology of suffering, it can seem like a lottery'. A third minister reflected:

> While the Lord has not healed me, despite prayers of many people at different times, I have found peace in the acceptance and reality of the Lord's reply to Paul, 'My grace is sufficient'. Many years ago my chest consultant commented that I should not humanly be able to do the things I did or take on the work load I was able to. And I worked for many years more after that. Healing may often be more in the mind and soul than in the body.

There can also be a cruel sense of failing family, friends and church, when they are praying for healing and the person fails to recover. Some people when close to death experience great distress from this sense of letting the side down. They may even come to dread visits from those friends from whom support might have been expected.

Of course we should pray for our friends, but physical healing does not always follow as the answer to fervent prayer. It is very hard to be told, as was a friend of mine, that you have not 'been healed' because her family and friends had not been praying in the 'right' way. Those who lead in healing ministry may be careful about their understanding and expectations, but simplistic interpretations abound. So many contributors have raised the pain they have experienced in this respect that it has to be mentioned here.

Where is God in all this?

Christians who have severe disabilities or whose children do are forced to think about their faith in a loving God. If they do not wrestle with this for themselves, friends will pose the questions. As Sally Nelson observed:

> Easily the question I have been asked most often since we discovered our daughter's needs is 'But what has it done to your faith?' I have been astonished at the number of Christians who have asked this question, as if our faith is indeed a delicate plant. We have responded with the conviction that this is what our faith is for: to make sense of life.

> ... I think we have lost confidence in our doctrine. In a consumer culture we feel the need to offer good stuff that passes the consumer test - and sin, suffering and disasters do not. In a search for a response I have looked back to Genesis 3, and asked myself whether I really expected to live out the consequences of the fall: maybe many of us Western Christians still need to undergo a *metanoia* regarding suffering ... There is a wealth of 'stuff' that we can use to teach about suffering, and stories touch the hurting heart better than undiluted doctrinal propositions.

In Victorian times, when death in childhood was common and when crippled children were a common sight, Christian journals were full of stories about faith against the odds. With improved medical care the incidence diminished in the twentieth century and the church seemed to forget how to speak into such situations. As I write

I am interrupted by a friend who is awaiting a probably grim diagnosis and tells me she is finding spiritual solace in a book that was her grandfather's about John Bunyan's blind daughter. The reluctance of many Christians today to grasp that faith is not an insurance policy for this life is strange. We worship a God who entered fully into the experience of human suffering.

* * * * *

Three personal reflections conclude this section. All three speak of special families who taught their disabled children to use their damaged limbs and whose love gave a healthy sense of self-worth and determination. These Christians have wrestled with 'the sharp end' of faith.

Paul Smith's difficult birth left him with cerebral palsy and a slight left hemiplegia (paralysis of one side of the body). Happily his twin sister was fully well. With great efforts all round he learned to walk and use his hands. In his late teens and early twenties he developed chronic pain in the lower back and left leg: the stress of achieving and maintaining mobility had permanently damaged his back and sciatic nerve. This was a cruel blow, but gradually he has been helped by drug therapy, a pain management course, and the love and prayers of friends.

My faith was deeply affected by the pain I experienced and there were many times when I felt deserted by God, and much I had been certain about came into question... When I first began to experience the pain problem, I had every confidence that it would respond to treatment. Gradually I realized that this was not going to happen and I was always facing disappointment after different treatments and the frustration of receiving temporary relief only to be set low again each time. This really tested my faith and, although I was unaware of it at the time, I began to get angry with God. Later, when I had come to terms with giving up part of my job and living a very restricted life, I became aware of my anger and resentment. I found it hard to accept the unpredictability of pain. This made life extremely difficult because it meant that I was unable to make any decisions or plans because I never knew when I might get an attack of pain.

There were times when I used to come home from a day's work so wracked with pain that I did not know what to do for the best. I did not want to be alone because I felt so isolated by the pain already, but I didn't feel able to be in anyone's company either because I felt so ill ... When I experienced acute pain that could go on for days, one of the hardest things was having to return to an empty home ... For that reason, it took me some time before I began to appreciate my own home and enjoy my own time. Friends would encourage me to stay at home and rest, and there were occasions when I did, but it was very important for me to get to work as I still needed to make my contribution. Constant pain and restriction can bring a huge feeling of worthlessness and uselessness. If I hadn't adopted what can be viewed as a hard attitude to myself and my problem, I believe I might have lost hold and given up completely.

He was helped by the presence and support of loving friends, who learned that they could do nothing to ease the pain yet could help just by being there, sitting and watching, and relieving the isolation.

He drew courage and strength from their presence. They remembered Jesus asking his disciples to watch and pray with him.

It taught me a lot about *dependence* on other people, how we need each other, and ultimately how we are dependent on God... There is sometimes an unwillingness within us to receive from others, far more than there is an unwillingness to give ... For those of us who experience handicap and illness there are times when we are faced with the inability to do those things which we can take for granted. There is the understandable embarrassment and sometimes pride at stake for us, and it can be difficult to come to terms with needing and asking for help. We do well to remember Our Lord's example of service and his disciples' lesson in receiving.

Sometimes we have to recognize that there are things beyond human control. This is something I learned as I came to terms with my pain.

What can the disabled person give to the church? It seems to me that disability is viewed negatively in society and within the church. People are seen for *what they cannot do* rather than for *what they can do* or for *who they are.* When will we begin to discover that people's lives can be enhanced by disability? Enhanced because people know the need to become united with the suffering Christ who shares in their pain, anger, frustration and loneliness and gives them companionship for the present and hope for the future ... People with disabilities can bring a distinctive ministry to the church, if we are prepared to invest in them.

Giles Murray led a full life, although born with cerebral palsy. After her death, her family found she written an account of her life and spiritual journey. Her husband and daughters kindly share this in the belief that she meant it to be used.

We are living in a world flawed, made imperfect by sin, and those of us who are obviously physically or mentally imperfect are so as a result of sin, but not, emphatically not, as a result of our own personal sinfulness, and usually not as a result of that of our parents... I do not believe that physical or mental disability is the punishment inflicted by a vengeful God as the result of breaking his laws.

In the story which John tells of the blind man cured on the Sabbath ... Jesus answered: 'His blindness has nothing to do with his sins or his parents' sins. He is blind so that God's power might be seen at work in him' - and then he cured the blind man. When I was younger, I used to think that the second sentence ... was rather heartless - almost as though God had caused the man to be born blind, to suffer sensory deprivation throughout his childhood and teenage years, to have to earn his living as a beggar, just so that Jesus could use him to demonstrate his power.

I have now come to view the whole story in a different light. We are all familiar with the statement that God hates the sin but loves the sinner, and I think this is another facet of that idea. When God allowed Adam and Eve to disobey him, he allowed the perfection of the world he had just created to be shattered. But he also paved the way for the most world-shattering events in time or eternity, the Incarnation, the Crucifixion, and the Resurrection, all three of which demonstrate a love for his creation and his creatures that is beyond our imagining. He hates sin, of course he does, because it is totally contrary to the perfection of his nature. He hates the results of sin, which are always travesties of the perfection of his creation. But the conversion, the re-turning to him voluntarily of one of his creatures through the acceptance of the sacrifice of his Son, is something which gives him great joy. We are made in his image, and it is one of Satan's choicest weapons to persuade us that that cannot be true if we are physically or mentally imperfect...

I believe categorically that the will of my heavenly Father, Creator of the Universe, for *all* his children is health, wholeness and perfection. I believe that he answers our prayers for healing in the same way, but not to the same degree, as he answers our prayers for forgiveness, because the health of our eternal souls is more important than the health of our physical bodies. My body is of the earth, earthy, and while I would enjoy having a body and limbs that behave 'normally', i.e. in the same way as the majority of other people, yet I cannot escape the conclusion that, although it is going to last me a lifetime, this is not my eternal dwelling. I believe that, because he has allowed me to be born with CP, he can use me with CP.

I most emphatically do not believe that he has *caused* me to be born with CP. It is not in the nature of the all-loving God who is my heavenly Father to cause pain to any of his children. Because I believe that my Father desires physical, mental and spiritual health for his children, and because his Son, my Saviour, spent so much of his spiritual energy healing the sick, I know I can bring my friends to him when they are ill or in pain, asking for his help. What I cannot *demand* or expect is their restoration to physical perfection or even to the stage they were at before, even as we cannot expect our own spiritual rehabilitation to restore us, this side of heaven, to the state of grace in which we would have been before the Fall.

I have been to 'Healing Services' ... I have not gone forward, nor will I, until the speaker calls specifically for a CP sufferer. That is when I will know that my Lord is expecting some physical improvement in me. Until then I will work for him as he has called me and where he has put me, however much I may shout at him for what I see as my inadequacies.

* * * * *

Craig Millward is the pastor of Ormesby Baptist Church. Thalidomide damage has given him two short arms and one usable hand.

I can't really say that I was greatly aware of the pain that living with my disability could cause until I was in my teens. Suddenly there came the embarrassment of being different, the isolation of being shunned, and the frustration of not being able to do things like everyone else. I suppose everyone copes with these things differently: my response was to be determined to do the things I could to the best of my ability, and let others get on with the rest. At that age it is the superficial things that are the most important, and it is only in later years that I have come to realize how a fiercely independent streak can make me less accessible to others, a desire to prove myself can lead me to become over-sensitive and perfectionist (which brings great frustration if it becomes impossible to do things to the high standards I set myself) and the fear of people's responses can have a paralysing effect in company.

I became a Christian at the age of fourteen. For the first few years my faith was at the affiliative stage. I was convinced that certain facts about God, Jesus and salvation were true, and I knew that I belonged to God. When I came to go to college, my faith began to deepen as I became more determined to put my beliefs into practice; but at the same time I became aware of a pain growing from within as some of the bigger questions began to burst onto the horizon.

Someone who grows up with a disability and a living faith in God can feel as if he is in the best of places and the worst of places all at once. On the one hand I was in touch with the God who is the only one who can bring healing to my inner hurts, and yet also within a church of loving and well-meaning people who, by trying to help me, reminded me that I was not the same as them. On the one hand, I was in relationship with a Father who loves me because I am truly created in his image, and yet was also forced to struggle with the painfully eternal questions of suffering that threatened to (and often did) put a barrier of anger and resentment between him and me.

In dealing with these questions I have discovered that, although I now have a number of rational and carefully reasoned answers to the problem of pain and suffering, none of them has really touched me at the centre of my being. What I have discovered, however, is that self-pity provides no answers, my mind provides a few and yet raises still more, whilst it is only as I have opened myself to

God and allowed him to pour himself into me that I have found anything that approaches wholeness. The most important thing I have learned is that, if my pain causes me to put a barrier up and begin to shake a fist at God, all I am doing is cutting myself off from the one who brings healing. But, strangely enough, it is not by searching for healing that I have found wholeness.

I believe in healing and am convinced that it should be part of the Church's normal ministry to the world. But my blackest time came after I came across the re-emergent healing ministry in a local church. The problem with that very early re-discovery was that it made the mistake of focusing upon healing and not on the Lord Jesus who sends his powerful Holy Spirit. I have come to understand that healing should begin with the Spirit who first communicates what he wishes to do and then does it as we pray. The greatest mistakes are made when we begin with what we see and what we feel God should do and are tempted to make promises to others on that basis. I need healing just as much as anyone else, and for the same kind of things. But I will only be made progressively whole as I present myself as an offering to God in praise and worship and with no preconditions. The danger of beginning with the symptoms we would like dealt with is that we risk having to face the faith-shattering conclusion that maybe the reason I have not been healed is that I am somehow second-class or lacking in faith. Thankfully, the healing ministry has grown up in recent years.

It is vital that people within our churches do two things when caring for disabled people. The first is to try and forget their differences when relating to them. I know what a compliment it is to have people tell me how amazed they are at the things I can do - but it does get wearing and simply reminds me that their expectation was that I would be able to do far less. But why? I've also had to endure numerous surprised faces when people discover I can be a Pastor and disabled at the same time. I have known people who have refused to take communion if I was breaking the bread, and another who felt I should not even be in Church because my disability was surely a sign that God was displeased with me or my parents! We must do our best to look past the disability and relate to disabled people as we would do to anyone else, since the hardest thing can be coping with the knowledge that you are 'different' and the feeling that different equals inferior.

At the same time I am asking that we also draw alongside a person with a disability and try to let a friendship develop. There may be things they will need to ask for help with and which, if they can ask a genuine friend, will not risk damaging their self-esteem or embarrassing them by making a 'big deal' out of it. It is also easier to discuss painful spiritual questions with friends. At the age of fourteen I had a group of really valuable friends who made integration into the church environment so much easier and I am still grateful to them to this day.

Part 2

TREAT WITH SPECIAL HONOUR
People with learning disabilities in the life of the Church

Those parts of the body that seem to be weaker are indispensable, and the parts that we think are less honourable we treat with special honour ... Now you are the body of Christ, and each one of you is a part of it.
1 Corinthians 12:22 - 3.27 NIV

Most people who have severe learning disabilities have limited ability to speak for themselves and need more articulate friends to speak on their behalf. Nevertheless, many find their own ways to communicate the comfort and joy they find in their faith. This section is, above all, a plea to churches to take seriously the challenge to share the Gospel with them and then to enable them to bring their own gifts to serve Christ and his church. Where special efforts are needed, those are one way of treating these apparently weaker brothers and sisters with special honour.

The challenge presented to the church by severe learning disability has an extra keen edge for Baptists. By delaying baptism and church membership until the candidate is capable of a deliberate, personal response to God, we sharpen the questions about those of limited intellectual understanding. Without actually imposing an intelligence test for believer's baptism, we wonder how to judge faith when conventional modes of communication fail. Traditionally Baptists have a 'high' view of the privileges and responsibilities of church membership, and they sometimes ask whether those with learning disabilities can understand enough for this. Sometimes it seems as if churches and ministers are more conscientious about testing candidates with disabilities against these Baptist principles than they are with other candidates. Experience, however, suggests that church members with learning disabilities are willing and reliable in tasks they are able to undertake and may attend meetings more regularly than many of those apparently better equipped to understand the proceedings.

Baptist principles highlight these questions: that is why Baptists have been prominent among pioneers in this field but, faced with severe learning disabilities, other churches have had similar hesitations about the formal reception of the baby, baptism, confirmation, full membership and access to the Lord's table, according to their particular practices. We share kindred concerns and can inform and encourage one another.

Let's face it: the majority of people are not immediately attracted to those who have learning disabilities. Many are unusual in appearance and manner, they may make alarmingly odd sounds or movements, they may dribble. Good Christians know better than to stare, of course, but it is easy to avert the gaze and pass by on the other side. Small residential homes 'in the community' may be a better idea than shutting people away in huge institutions - but we would rather they were not in our backyard! Those who resist such temptation and try to be friendly soon discover that communication can be quite difficult. Happily, more and more Christians are rising to the challenge of getting to know disabled people and discovering that this can be a truly rewarding field of ministry.

Richard's Story

The second child of a Christian family, he was conceived in love and enfolded in prayer. Pregnancy went smoothly but at birth he was found to have Down's Syndrome, a genetic abnormality present from conception. In those days the parents' relative youth had spared them antenatal testing and the cruel choice over abortion. Had he died in the first weeks, they would have felt relief, but the baby's hold on life proved strong, without the organic defects often associated with the Syndrome. His parents, of academic inclination and prizing intelligence, were appalled at the prospect of intellectual impairment. At the dedication service, thanksgiving was muted. The parents silently prayed that somehow God would make his life useful. They also became keenly aware that their church was taking this child to heart in a special way. When that afternoon Richard produced his first real smiles, that early sign of deliberate mental response, it did not seem coincidence.

The parents needed the church's support over the pre-school years, when the 'experts' seemed determined to dismiss every hopeful sign of development. The paediatrician who examined Richard in the first week offered a bleak prognosis for a Down's child - well below what is now seen as likely achievement. Probably the doctors' experience was limited to those in institutional care, with limited stimulation and correspondingly low expectation, but their constant discouragement was hard to handle.

Slowly Richard made progress. Often he first achieved new things at church. With so many protective eyes on him, he was allowed more freedom in the church hall than in other spacious places and this seemed to liberate him to new efforts. He moved up the Sunday School, mostly with a slightly younger age group - but there was anyway a dearth of boys of his own age. Doubtless he was sometimes difficult, but teachers and children coped, and *no-one complained to his parents*. An obliging habit of dozing off when bored helped: it was to stand him in good stead later during sermons! Now he insists he does not sleep in church but copes with sermons by praying for the assembled company - that is why his eyes are closed!

For Richard, the atmosphere of the church has always been one of welcome and friendship, and he soon loved the house of the Lord. The elderly widow of the former minister introduced him early to Christian service: going round to collect empty coffee cups, she enlisted the tiny child's help to save her bending to the lower shelf of the trolley. The mother treasured in her heart such evidence of her child's worth.

When nearly five, Richard began to recognize words on 'flash cards', but educational psychologists told his parents off since, being Down's, he 'would never read with understanding'. Belonging to a bookish family, he was interested in reading and school teachers proved more optimistic.

At school, number work never appealed to him. Whatever colourful equipment appeared, Richard registered 'sums', cradled his head on his arm and dozed off. Helping with coffee at church was different: a kind friend taught him to take small payments and count out change. Other caterers later taught the rudiments of division - in cutting cakes into the requisite number of portions. Where learning is laborious, it helps to see some point in it!

The day came when the minister told the parents that Richard, then aged sixteen, had asked her to take him in the water because he loved Jesus. After a period of careful preparation, which proved a learning experience and a delight to candidate and minister alike, he was baptized as a believer and received into full membership of the church. Over two succeeding decades he has proved a responsible, active member and the church has encouraged this, patiently allowing him to learn new tasks, a slow but ultimately rewarding effort.

By the time he left school Richard could read fairly well and write a little. These hard-won skills might easily have been lost without a compelling reason to exercise them - parental prompting would never have sufficed. Ongoing Bible studies with the ministers, tailored to his needs, provided splendid incentive. He now reads with considerable fluency, which helps in many aspects of life.

For someone with a good reading vocabulary but limited concentration span, the Bible has a great advantage: whole stories are often contained in a few lines! Richard loves to be given references to look up. Books of prayers and hymns also come in bite-sized chunks. He spends happy hours assembling his own devotional material, including recorded songs, around given themes.

Richard's speech is passably fluent, though he tends to grab at key words rather than listen to whole sentences, so communication can be patchy. Like many such people, he is alert to body language and this helps him relate well to people. In a church that always has visitors in the congregation, he has developed his own effective ways of making people welcome.

He is quick to detect any particular need, whether for a supportive arm on steps, a cup of tea, or a pastoral conversation. The physical needs he will meet himself, and find someone appropriate for deeper conversations. Once he drew his mother's attention to an occasional visitor who looked her usual smartly dressed self. 'Mum, go and talk to that lady - she is crying inside'. It transpired that her husband had died that week and she could not face the massed sympathy of her own church, yet needed someone with whom to share her grief. She was indeed crying inside.

Richard is aware that churches differ in style, but he has no difficulty in recognizing their common faith and fellowship. *Songs of Praise*, regularly recorded for him to watch after church, has made him familiar with a range of worship styles. He loves his own church dearly but is also comfortable in the parish church, and has formed links with two other local Baptist fellowships, helping for some years with a senior citizens' lunch club at one, and delighting in the other's special midweek worship group for people with learning and other disabilities.

Richard comes into his own at church - and, indeed, in any gathering of Christians. This is the context in which he lives most abundantly. He takes his turn on the stewarding rota and is always ready to plug gaps. He welcomes visitors and runs errands. He helps with catering, bakes cakes for parties, and is always ready to jump up and make people tea and coffee. He distributes the *Baptist Times*, folds leaflets and stuffs envelopes. He joins in periodic workdays around the premises. He keeps a protective eye on adventurous toddlers, and enjoys his annual appearance as Father Christmas. He knows his way around the nooks and crannies of the Victorian chapel better than many members and is often sent to find things or put them away. All this is best expressed when he receives the people's offering and presents that to the minister - for him, always a priestly act as he represents the people before God.

Richard is my son and it is his love of Jesus and his enjoyment of everything connected with the church that daily renews my zeal to encourage churches to be open to such people and help more of them to receive the glad news that God's love embraces them, just as they are.

The Challenge of Learning Disabilities

'Learning disabilities' cover a wide range of conditions. They may have a genetic cause, or be the result of damage at birth or early childhood illness or accident. In Britain the term *learning disability* is used to cover a wide range of conditions (in the USA it is applied more narrowly to conditions that affect education, like dyslexia and visual and auditory processing disorders, but not the full range of what is there called mental retardation or developmental disability). The approved terminology in this field tends to have a short life, too often degenerating into general terms of abuse: *idiot* and *imbecile* were once technical definitions. When the BUild work began, the term *mental handicap* was still widely used, but this was easily confused with mental illness, and the language of handicap was being discouraged.

In July 2008 the Foundation for Learning Disabilities reported that 985,000 people in England have a learning disability: 2% of the population. Many of these have mild or moderate disabilities (IQs in the 50 to 70 range), but a fifth of them will be more severely or even profoundly disabled. Many come from socially disadvantaged backgrounds, since poverty and poor environment can contribute to the condition in the first place, while care for the child with serious disability will normally reduce a family's earning capacity. Only 17% of adults with learning disability have paid work themselves, and usually that is only part-time and low paid.

Low income is only one factor in a wider spectrum of people with learning disabilities seeming to matter less to society at large than people of greater ability. Only a few days before I revised this passage in August 2008, a report drew attention to the poorer attention they often receive from medical services in Britain. Attitudes to disability have improved considerably in recent years, but there is still some way to go. Valerie Sinason, a psychoanalytical psychotherapist, has observed that

> Where something is seriously wrong that cannot be repaired we often seem to be reminded of our mental and physical frailty and mortality. This leads to some of the most inspired preventative or reparative work on the one hand or to blaming, scapegoating, disowning on the other ... At the most extreme end ... the damaged child is written off as ... pre-human and therefore the value of his or her life is under threat. Devalued children and adults have ... eceived the worst services.
>
> *Mental Handicap and the Human Condition*
> London 1992, pp.10-12

Such language rings challenging bells for the church. Our Christian antennae should be alert, since we assert that *all* are of *equal* value in God's eyes. We know that Jesus had a special care for the disadvantaged and marginalized. We are sure that he would treat people with learning disabilities with special honour, just as he did the poor, the outcast, the physically disabled and the mentally ill. He would never write off the damaged child as without value, but human society often does just that, even if it does not express it so bluntly.

People fondly imagine that those with learning disabilities will not notice, will not understand that they are different, will not grasp that they are treated as lesser beings. My experience has been that most are well aware of this. Sinason, used to more severely disabled children than am I, confirms this. She tells of a child who lifted a doll's hair and pointed to the head beneath:

'Gone wrong', she said, 'right from the root'. She knew, as every handicapped child and adult I have ever seen knew, that she was different. She also knew that she felt the difference was not a good difference but was a sign of something having gone biologically wrong ... There is the struggle of feeling part of a flawed creation, 'children of a lesser god'.

Mental Handicap and the Human Condition, p.60

These feelings are often shared by the parents, and Christians need to respond with something more robust than sentimental kindness if they are going to help those closely involved with such disability to grasp that God loves and values them all.

Listen to a young woman, Viv Simmonds, explaining what it is like and appreciating those who treat her *'like a person':.*

What do I mean, 'they treat me as a person'? I mean they don't put me in a box with a label and they don't talk down to me. I can relax with some people and be myself because they see 'me'. I don't really feel I'm handicapped and I want to have relationships the same as everyone else... I wear a hearing aid which sometimes 'goes on the blink' ... Sometimes I get my words mixed up. I don't mind if people laugh when I do this. I laugh myself and, if others can laugh too, we'll laugh together and understand each other much better. I know the Lord loves me and accepts me as I am ... I love talking to the Lord and I pray for many people. I like people to ask me to pray for them and I never forget ... Our pastor says that if we had to pass an exam to get into heaven, none of us would make it, but I would still like to know what it's like to get 'A' levels and go to college...

I'm learning with difficulty and thank God for all the things
I can do.

Relatively few people with learning disabilities can be so
articulate about it, but many would echo Viv's delight in prayer. It is
often apparent that they find talking to Jesus easy - the one friend
who does not struggle to understand their speech. I remember being
moved by one devout man's long and impassioned prayer which
sounded to me like a series of grunts, punctuated regularly with the
one clear phrase 'Praise the Lord', and terminating with a clear
'Amen'.

This book is intended to help churches proclaim and
demonstrate the love of God who accepts people as they are.

Effects of disabling conditions

Some of the causes of learning disability fall into distinct groups with recognizable characteristics. These are often described as particular syndromes, Down's Syndrome being the most common, while some occur very rarely. Knowing something about a condition may help, and it is easy these days to get information off the web just by googling the relevant term.

There is, however, a real danger of stereotyping. It is all too easy to see the condition and overlook the individual. The parents of a child with Down's Syndrome, a condition easily recognized by typical physical attributes, can get rather tired of being told their child is therefore loving, sociable and musical. I used to feel that people wanted to write off Richard's nicer traits as part of the condition, whereas I saw the stubbornness and maddening ability to 'switch off' from all external stimuli as typical of his condition. Relatives lose their identity too and become 'the mother of that Down's boy' or 'the funny girl's brother'. If you want to be truly helpful there is no substitute for getting to know the individual, making allowance for the condition but not only seeing the person through that lens. Thinking of them by name rather than by condition is a good start, giving an immediate individual identity.

Personal names are important to people with learning disabilities. Many with very little speech will tell you their name and ask yours. Names are important to God too, remember Isaish 43.1: 'I call you by name; you are mine.'

If you want to befriend people who have learning disabilities, mild or severe, you need to know them individually. You need to understand what they can do and what is difficult for them. You need to find out what will help them most. They may not be able to tell you themselves. Parents or the regular care-givers can usually explain particular needs.

I have been touched by the instinctive way Richard's eldest nephew has understood this. My elder son insisted from Tim's birth that the baby should be entrusted to Richard as a responsible adult, and Richard has had a special love for this child. He could share in the care of Tim and his brothers, and in physical play, but could engage less when they moved to intricate Lego constructions and highly imaginative games. When Tim was about nine he came to me quietly to ask about Richard's patchy ability. He wanted to know what was particularly difficult for his uncle and therefore how better to involve him. How should he explain games? He could readily grasp that it was best to *show* rather than *tell* Richard how to do something. Tim is now twelve and I have enjoyed watching Richard teach Tim to play snooker and Tim teach Richard to play various computer games. Tim told me, 'I know Uncle Richard won't like zapping people, so I've found others he'll find more interesting.'

Most people who have severe learning disabilities have problems with communication. Many have little or no spoken language, but they may use sign language, gestures and mime effectively. Others may have apparently fluent speech but that may mask considerable difficulty in understanding by word *alone*. Many will keep repeating information once they have mastered that particular vocabulary - an apparently sensible conversation loses something when heard several times! Some know what they want to say but getting it out in words may be a slow process. Poor communication is terribly frustrating and will underlie some of the behavioural problems often associated with learning disabilities. The surprising thing is how many are actually cheerful, well-balanced people!

A lot of people with learning disabilities find a clear structure to their day or week helpful and, particularly with children or non-verbal people, a series of simple pictures giving a simple 'time-table' can help guide them through with less anxiety. For example, a Sunday school class might show symbols for greeting, prayer, music, the Bible, drawing or craft work to show the planned sequence of activities, perhaps ending with the time for a drink. For those who feel safe with routine and who cannot tell the time, such aids can be a real help.

Disabling conditions are complex. The more severe the learning disability, the greater the likelihood of physical and sensory impairments as well. Epilepsy may add to the difficulties. Genetic abnormalities present from conception often affect organs and limbs as well as ability to learn; often these present a characteristic outward appearance. Damage to the brain at birth or later, often less easily identified, may result in particular or multiple disability.

Some conditions run in families. It has long been recognized that haemophilia and colour blindness are passed down within families, but now it is clear that various other conditions may be inherited in this way. Some conditions affect only one sex, or jump a generation, others recur more randomly. It is bad enough to grasp that one's son is severely disabled without having to accept at the same time that his sister is likely to carry the condition to her children. Genetic testing can often determine who are carriers - which is good for those who prove to be in the clear! Many families now know they are 'sitting on a time-bomb', as one father put it. Testing is not always accurate and false alarms or reassurances are not unknown, both difficult for parents.

This book cannot give a comprehensive guide to recognizable conditions which might be met in churches, but describing a few may give some idea of the complex possibilities.

Down's Syndrome

This is a well-known genetic variation with distinctive physical characteristics, particularly apparent in the face. It is caused by an extra chromosome and the most common forms occur randomly, although one variant recurs in families. Older mothers are more prone to produce Down's babies. Many people who have Down's Syndrome are short and have very short fingers, which is restricting in itself. Even the whorls of the fingerprints are distinctively different, and one of the usual two creases across the palm is normally absent. Heart malformations are common. Many are particularly susceptible to respiratory infections. The condition can now be detected in early pregnancy, so many Down's foetuses are aborted. Churches that take a pro-life stance ought to be especially vigilant in support of parents who choose to bear a child who is expected to have disabilities.

Compared with other disabilities, people with Down's Syndrome are relatively fortunate. The condition is visible and easily recognized, so people make allowances. Most are sociable and relate well to other people, in spite of speech problems. It is not usually difficult to relate to them - though their ready hugs may be overwhelming!

There is some truth in the stereotype of happy, loving people with a love of music - but it is a pity to write off a person's more attractive characteristics as just part of the syndrome! Some, alas, are not happy and sociable. Most can be stubborn, probably because it is such an effort to understand and co-operate. They may have these similarities, but they are not clones: they have their own characters and their own experience of life.

To make up for lack or inadequacies of speech, many people with Down's have a real gift for acting, probably because they are extra alert to body language. They can be very funny and enjoy making people laugh. In groups of disabled people, those with

Down's often help to get things going with a swing. It seems sad that this condition is now one of the easiest to eliminate: their disappearance would considerably impoverish the world of other people with disabilities and of many beyond.

Other recognizable genetic syndromes, each with its own characteristics, include, for example:

Fragile X Syndrome

This syndrome was only identified in 1970 but occurs quite often. It covers a family of genetic conditions, all relating to changes in one particular gene. It probably accounts for much of what was once seen as non-specific disability, and is the most common *inherited* cause of mental impairment, so tends to run in families. Identification of a genetic cause and recognizable characteristics can help families and teachers to assist affected children. For example, they usually avoid eye contact and often take things in better from someone standing behind them. They often get on well with computer learning programmes.

Sotos Syndrome

In this rare genetic condition the head and body grow large while the mind develops slowly. One father described his five-year-old son as looking nine while having the mind of a two-year-old. He had a lovely smile but was unstable on his feet, doubly incontinent, had feeding difficulties, dribbled and was often sick without warning. His loving father had revised his idea of hell since his days in theological college: now it was taking his son round the supermarket or realizing that he was being sick in the local swimming pool. A mother remembered the time her child managed to plunge the whole of

Woolworths into darkness, stop an escalator, turn a street light on, walk around on a tray of cream cakes, press a security alarm bell, and, in hospital for tests, demolish two trolleys full of sterilized instruments. Both these parents commented on the times they have been asked, 'How do you cope?'

There are a other recognized syndromes causing learning disability, as well as the conditions attributed to brain damage, often the result of a difficult birth or subsequent damage by disease or accident. This makes it hard to generalize. There is no substitute for getting to know the individuals you encounter.

Behavioural problems

Difficult behaviour is often associated with severe learning disabilities, whatever the specific diagnosis. Some of it relates to the inability to communicate what they want or would like to do, and the resultant frustration.

Many parents - and all too often it is left to mothers alone - cope because they love their children and they have little choice. They cope on little sleep because such children often have very disturbed nights. They rise to change and wash the bed linen and try to keep one step ahead, averting disaster through the coming day. It is not surprising that many families become cut off from normal life around them. Few friends understand the pressures, the struggle to maintain any 'normal' life and the resultant isolation.

Autism and Asperger's Syndrome

Autism and Asperger's are words heard a lot more these days as more people become aware of them due to the media, internet and television programmes. It is a myth to say that someone has autistic tendencies: people are diagnosed with either autism or Asperger's. These conditions affect the way the brain processes information and how those affected communicate and relate to other people.

The spectrum of the disorder is vast and ranges from the very profound who need a lot of support to access everyday activities to those of high intelligence who will lead full independent lives. Asperger's is considered by most experts to fall within the autistic spectrum, although people with Asperger's tend to be more able. Autism affects both sexes but is more prevalent in boys.

Autism has been described as 'an invisible barrier' erected between the person affected and other people. Most look 'normal'. Some seem able to absorb lots of information but lack the ability to sort it out. Some will try to converse but may easily drift on to unrelated topics. It is difficult to hold a two-way conversation about anything and this probably encourages withdrawal, or they may focus exclusively on one topic which is their current interest to the exclusion of all else. Others with learning disabilities often fix on something that has taken their interest and may like to revert to the safe, familiar topic but not usually in the exclusive way of those with autism.

People with Autism or Asperger's will have problems with *communication, imagination* and *socialization;* this is restricting in what we would think of as normal functions. They like things to be ordered and can become obsessive about all sorts of things, like routine, how they wear their cloths, where and how things are kept, even how cutlery is placed on the table.

It is important for people with autism or Asperger's to have clear, well-defined timetables, routines and schedules. This reduces anxiety and allows the person to function more easily. Too much stimulation or excitement adds to their difficulty in unscrambling information. Variation from their norm can result in behavioural problems causing enormous problems for everyone. This can be difficult to cope with. It is always useful to talk to parents or carers for advice on how the person likes things done and how best to deal with their behaviour.

A Baptist minister whose son has autism and who has had experience of a number of people with autism and Asperger's in his church has suggested that their characteristics are almost as contrary as they can be from those of the church - and yet some find a welcoming home there.

The person with autism may sometimes make gestures that are repeated, like looking at their hands and twiddling the fingers, playing with the wheels of a toy car rather than driving it along, repeating words, even hitting themselves. One young man had been on a drama course where his part required him to shout out a word that was really not suitable in a lot of circumstances. Thereafter, every time he was in a situation where he felt threatened, he would shout out this word repeatedly. He would also do it when he wanted attention. It is important always to consider well what you say and teach!

Communication

This can be difficult but is important. It helps to know which communication system the person uses. Various methods are used and these can vary from county to county. Finding the best way to communicate with the people you deal with is important, especially when trying to help them find helpful order in a given situation or activity.

Makaton symbols and signs - can be broken down to small activities: cleaning teeth, going out - and where to, etc. Some will need to be given one symbol at a time, while others will cope with a small book holding a series of movable symbols. As each is used, it can be moved to the back of the book, marking progress.

Pictures - can be used to show who they will be meeting or what they will be doing during the day. Thus, if the person is going to church, a picture of the church will be shown to them. There is also a picture exchange system where the person gives the picture to show what they want. For example, a picture of a Big Mac given to the assistant in MacDonalds is an alternative way to ask for the food instead of having to speak. This can help the non-verbal person and take the anxiety out of the situation.

Such aids can be used with verbal prompts but, if that causes stress, then use only the signals and signs.

Pat Maisch draws on her own experience and on Shopler and Mesibov, 'High Functioning Individuals with Autism', to offer advice for speaking to someone with Autism or Asperger's:

Voice should be calm, persistent, and of even tone.
Manner should be firm, no-nonsense, steady and matter-of-fact.
Posture should be non-threatening, firm, in charge, in close proximity without crowding.
Words should be kept to a minimum. Any unnecessary words should be eliminated. Language should be positive, matter-of-fact, concrete, and definitive.
Phrasing should be simple and direct. Use the future conditional:'When you are sitting calmly, then I will discuss it with you'.

Tone should be calm and patient (even through clenched teeth!)

Respect the person with autism as you would respect everyone else.

It is important to be clear, precise, confident and positive in what you say. When organizing activities for someone with autism or Aspergers, keep directions clear and precise and have a clear beginning and end to the activity. Give advance warning that 'in five minutes we will finish'. Always give as much praise as possible - even if you would not normally do so.

Imagination

People with autism or Asperger's have problems in this area. They take everything literally so it is important not to use metaphors or idiosyncratic phrases when speaking to them. It is unrealistic to expect them to use imagination. Two illustrations will help to show how careful you need to be.

A young man with autism was in the Young People's Department of the Sunday School. The leader brought in a variety of items, gave one to each of the young people and asked them to think of something that their object could be used for other than its main intended purpose. When he asked the young man what he could use the coat hanger for, the reply was 'to hang your clothes on'. The leader made some suggestions, but the answer was always the same: the coat hanger is for hanging clothes on!

A young man was living in a care home, but he was quite capable of going out on his own. One of the carers asked if he could do something for him. 'Yes' was the reply. 'Can you post me a letter?' Again the answer was 'Yes'. 'Do you know where the letter box is?' 'Yes', again came the reply and off he went to post the letter. The Post Office was only a five-minute walk from the home. Two hours went by and the young man had not returned. The staff had gone out to look for him in vain and were about to call the police when he returned home. On questioning him, the staff learned he had posted the letter at the person's home address. He had walked across the town to the address on the envelope and posted it through the door.

What the member of staff should have said to him was, 'Can you do a job for me? Take this letter and put it in the post box at the Post Office.'

Socialization

People with autism and Asperger's find difficulty with socialization and will often be found on the outside of a group or on their own. They find eye contact difficult and are not keen on people getting too close to them. Being in unfamiliar places can cause anxiety; new places, new people and new activities may need to be introduced slowly over a period time.

Gradually the person can learn to trust you and become easier to work with. Accept such people as the invididuals they are, recognize that they can take a long time to get used to changes, always be consistent in what you do and say. The use of photographs, both of people and places before visits, may help.

You may be the one that will have to change - your attitude, the way you talk, even how close you normally stand to another person.

'I feel I belong'

One father is often amazed at what his adult son who has autism can do: he is good with his hands, enjoys pottery, and likes his part-time job. He travels alone competently, even abroad. He absorbs information but cannot unscramble it logically for any length of time. Any conversation is hard work so he soon goes off on his own again. Yet he is extrovert and enjoys group activities, like outings, a skittles evening, a beetle drive. He is sociable yet isolated, unable to make any real friends. He loves going to church and his parents feel there is a spiritual quality to his life and a trusting faith, but it is hard to pin it down. He is able to read the Bible well in worship. At a BUild conference he offered to tell a group session about his baptism, describing this in enthusiastic detail, right down to who held his eye-glasses while he was immersed.

Yet he cannot easily show any feelings: his emotions are trapped behind that unseen barrier. His parents watch for the rare opportunities to 'get through' to him. Most people, even in a friendly and accepting church, keep at a certain distance. 'You cannot get to know him', says his father sadly. 'You feel there is a real person behind that barrier but he cannot release it and you just don't know what there is to know there.' Yet this man told us how he loves going to a home group although he rarely contributes to the discussion. 'I feel I belong', he said: surely a significant statement for such a man.

Some manage to penetrate the barrier a little and reach out for contact, helping others to glimpse something of their inner turmoil. Sue Norris, an active supporter of BUild, wrote, 'not a lot of people understand me'. For her, life is often terrible, but she loves God. Sue kindly shares her poem, 'Inner Light', to help readers understand a little more.

I saw my inner light
when I was seen darkly.
I found joy in grim things
from the nothings
which became everythings
filling my heart with love
when I was looking empty.
I had the most glowing light
which is something given,
given by the inner light soul me
where God shines the most,
I rest play and work
surrounded by my inner light.

Example of the effects of Asperger's Syndrome

From experience with her son, Sue Houghton adds further examples relating to Asperger's Syndrome (AS).

Most people who have AS are intelligent, often very intelligent. They know that they are 'different' and want to 'be liked' by others, to have friends, including a boy or girl friend, and a job; sadly, these 'normal' desires may be frustrated or fraught with difficulty.

Usually they have good verbal communication yet may have difficulty with a two-way conversation. They may tend to talk *at* you rather than to you, and may focus on their own experience and beliefs with little interest in the views of other people. Confusion and misunderstandings arise when they take everything literally. Passing a local shop which had changed hands and now bore the sign

'Mortgage Doctor', Sue had difficulty explaining this to her son when he protested that you cannot take a house to the doctor!

Joining in social events may well appeal to the person with AS although poor social skills make interaction difficult. Much preparation will be needed if going to an unfamiliar venue as the familiar and routine are important aids. People with AS find it incredibly hard to understand non-verbal signals, including facial expressions, which complicates attempts to form and maintain relationships. Most people with AS will not be able to tolerate certain sounds, especially sudden loud noises.

Often they develop an obsessive interest in a hobby or in collecting something. Limited development of interpersonal play and imagination often results in repetitive watching of the same DVD or careful lining or stacking up the same toys or other items to perfection. It may be possible to make a positive virtue of the particular interest and aptitude, especially in adult life. Gathering facts and figures tends to come easily and this can be useful in study or specialist areas of employment.

Family life can be complicated as they like a clear order to their day and find change difficult. With their liking for routine however, and their precision over times and dates, they are usually well organized and that can be a plus for employment. After all, they would never be late for work and probably never want to take a day off work!

BUild

The Baptist Union Initiative with people with learning disabilities began when two church workers wanted to help children with limited general understanding learn about God's love. The education officer of the Baptist Union of Great Britain, Bryan George, arranged a meeting in London in November 1983 for anyone concerned about ministry with people who had what were then called mental handicaps. Community care policies were then coming into effect: it was clear that with the closure of the large, isolated hospitals, which had been the main provision since Victorian times, far more people with severe learning disabilities would soon be seen in local communities. Would churches welcome them? Would Christians help them to settle in?

A working group was formed and began to gather information, discovering what experience churches already had and sharing this to encourage others. The *Baptist Times'* help was invaluable in these early contacts. At first pastoral concerns were dominant, but there were underlying questions of theological understanding, and always that desire to make the Gospel accessible to people who had learning disabilities. The work has been supported by people from many different churches, within the Baptist denomination and beyond. It has claimed the enthusiasm and practical service of some of our leading thinkers, and has revealed much unselfish care and, perhaps more surprising, deep theological understanding among 'ordinary' church members.

Members of the BUild working group have given talks and produced articles and books (Bryan George, *The Almond Tree*, Collins Liturgical, 1987; Faith Bowers, *Let Love Be Genuine*, BUGB 1985; *Who's this sitting in my pew?* SPCK Triangle, 1988; and *Treat with special honour*, BUGB, 1997). An early publication was a set of four teaching booklets for use with baptismal candidates, *Knowing Jesus, Following Jesus, The Church, Joining the Church* (Susan Wright, Ena Robertson and Faith Bowers, BUGB 1991). Further special teaching materials have followed, including *The Lord's Prayer,* with the traditional words, a simple paraphrase, and a picture for each clause, and Siôr Coleman's, *Friends of Jesus* (BUGB 2002), which introduces some Christian figures down the ages. Further materials are being prepared.

BUild also produces a newsletter and has arranged day conferences around the country to encourage and help churches with such ministry. Increasingly, people with learning disabilities have themselves taken a leading part in these conferences. On one occasion actors with special needs from Harlow led a Baptist Assembly with their re-enactments of the Good Samaritan parable and the passion of Christ. At another Assembly a group gathered together on the day gave a musical presentation during the evening session.

In 1996 nine people from BUild ran a summer camp in Poland to introduce Baptists there to this area of ministry. These camps were repeated in subsequent years and training and equipment given so that now Polish Baptists are able to continue and extend this ministry themselves. Other contacts made initially through BUild have led to the group in Harlow giving much support, practical and inspirational, to those running an orphanage for children with severe disabilities in Poland. These 'small candles' shine out in the darkness where little had been done to enhance the lives of such people and those who care for them. In time the striking results of good practice and more stimulation are likely to be observed and copied more widely. There has been some contact with churches in Bulgaria and Kosova, again raising concern for those with severe disabilities, but BUild does not have the personnel to undertake a lot there.

BUild early recognized the need to address theological issues. Many people who do not naturally think theologically wrestle with big questions when they have a child who has disabilities. Often pastors have not been ready for this. When BUild has arranged theological consultations, a surprising range of Christians have travelled considerable distances to take part. Learned theologians have rubbed shoulders with the searing pain and determined faith of parents. While never comfortable occasions, these can be times of real blessing.

Much of the achievement stems from the way BUild has drawn together in shared concern a wide mix of people. This was particularly striking in the early years of the group. It is a rare forum where relatives of the disabled, carers, ministers, voluntary church workers, professionals from health, social services and education, and, increasingly, people with disabilities themselves have come together *on the same side of the table*. The secular world is good at dividing these into different and too often opposing groups, but in Christ all meet on an equal footing and that gives new perspectives and opportunities.

Churches open to people with learning disabilities tell how this opens doors to wider mission. When the church is seen to get involved with those for whom many feel sorry - from a safe distance - it wins the respect of local citizens. Social services, who find it hard to get those in their care accepted in the community, warm to churches that welcome them and have staying power.

In 1984 a BUild survey of churches found only a quarter had any direct experience of mental handicap, though many ministers were prepared to envisage positive responses if it were to come their way. Today there is far more real experience and often unexpected enthusiasm. One church that supported the idea of residential homes nearby explained, 'We had a pastoral role in quieting community fears born of ignorance. Our ties with these fine young people are strong.' Elsewhere ten residents from a local home came to the church: 'We are constantly challenged and encouraged by the ready interest of each in the mainstream life of the church.' One minister wrote of the contribution of two young people: 'The naturalness and openness of their faith and love for the Lord is a real challenge to the clutter of our churchy faith!' Another goes so far as to declare from his experience: 'People with learning disabilities make the best evangelists!'

Sue Houghton, a member of the BUild committee, was persuaded to go to church by her own son who has severe disabilities but who kept telling her about Jesus. He had first gone to the church for Boys' Brigade which had welcomed and included a little boy when, among other disabilities, he had not yet acquired any speech.

Certainly our friends with learning disabilities have fewer inhibitions than most of us and are less likely to make convenient cultural distinctions about where and when to speak of their faith. 'Are you a Christian?' the young man asks the friendly theatre assistant, who apologetically confesses she is not. 'That's a pity', he observes sadly, wanting to share the joy of Christian fellowship. And why not openly give thanks before tucking into the MacDonald's burger or the picnic in the park? They may not be able to discuss their faith in detail, but they show how much it is part of their lives.

Disability in God's Creation

Making the Word flesh

The Bible has little to say about learning disabilities. Few with severe conditions would have survived long in the ancient world, while those mildly affected would have been absorbed more easily into 'low tech', labour-intensive communities. Both Old and New Testaments, however, firmly make room for other marginalized minorities, proclaiming the need for compassion and justice. Jesus claims just such a proclamation as his personal 'mission statement' (Isaiah 1.1-2; Luke 4.18-19).

Christians generally do not doubt that God's love must encompass those with learning disabilities. It is the adequacy of the response of Christian men and women that is open to question, and our readiness to recognize that people with severe learning disabilities are themselves capable of responding to God's love.

The essential humanity of such people needs to be affirmed. Because they differ from the human 'norm', their very humanness is often questioned, albeit silently. However kindly meant, the common perceptions of such people as 'God's holy innocents' - 'incapable of sin' - denies their full humanity. As a Mencap poster put it, 'They may not think as quickly but they feel as deeply'. Most have some understanding of right and wrong, and experience the range of human emotions, even if these are not expressed in words. They know about praise and blame, encouragement and disapproval, inclusion and rejection, and often have all too much experience of the unhappier alternatives. Recognizing this affirms their humanity and challenges the church to rise to more than sentimental kindness.

We so often interpret the *goodness* of God's creation as our concept of *perfection*, without blemish, and are bewildered when faced with those born with apparently great imperfections. We may live in a fallen world, but we still look for perfection in each new act of creation - the dawn light, the rose bud, the new baby. Perhaps we need to adjust our perspectives. As a sharp-eyed child, I used to delight friends by finding four-leaf clover. I already understood that they were a genetic aberration - like Down's Syndrome - but those leaves were seen by many as 'lucky', special in a desirable way.

Those who have real limitations when it comes to learning through the intellect, by words and reasoning, are often better able to learn through their senses and emotions. *They need the Word made flesh.* Does the church reflect enough on the legacy of being Christ's body, continuing to be broken in order to flesh out the Word? In receiving the bread and wine, the church is surely called to be vulnerable with Christ. Faced with learning disabilities, Christians may well feel vulnerable, at a loss when speech, the usual means of communication, proves of little use. But they still have a Gospel to proclaim.

When words convey less than facial expressions, gestures, the whole demeanour, we need to present the Gospel of Christ with our whole bodies. The willingness of Christians to make special efforts for those who are accustomed to being despised and rejected is in itself Gospel proclamation. God's love is revealed through those who own him as Lord. Jean Vanier, who chose to live with two disabled friends and out of that experience founded the L'Arche communities, has observed, 'Loving someone is not doing things for them but revealing to them that they are precious.'

Grasping this should affect our dealings with people of *all* abilities, for most find learning easier when words are reinforced with sensory aids and delivered by someone manifestly enthusiastic for the subject. To proclaim the love of God, we should first 'let the Word of Christ dwell in us richly' (Colossians 3.16). As members of his body, we become Christ's audio-visual aids.

The impact on people with learning disabilties of grasping that God loves them - just as they are - can be dramatic. So often they are aware of disappointing those who love them and long to see them achieve a little more. The liberating, unconditional affirmation of them as the people they are brings new confidence and happiness.

It is easy to think of their faith as 'simple', not having to struggle with intellectual doubts, yet it may be hard won, refined in the painful crucible of 'being different'. Such faith, even if not articulated in words, can release into the church and world an unexpected mission force, finding new ways to express the impact of God's love. This can be humbling and challenging to the church's usual perceptions. The church, being full of humans, becomes set in its ways. The church, being of God, may sometimes 'turn the world upside-down'. 'To shame what is strong, God has chosen what the world counts weakness' (1 Corinthians 1.25-31).

The potential of grace

Arising from contact between the Baptist Union of Poland with the East Glamorganshire English Baptist Association, David Clark, a Baptist minister, visited Poland on several occasions to help Christians there explore what they could do for people with severe disabilities. This reflection comes from a sermon David preached in Poland.

'And God saw everything that he had made and behold it was very good' (Gen.1.31) - God's eyesight is very different from ours. God can see beauty where there is none. God can even embrace the Cross. Isaiah 53.2 has been translated this way: 'He was so disfigured, he hardly looked human'. We Christians have dared to take that passage for our own, as an apt description of our Saviour who went down the road to death so that no one should cry in vain for the light of his face. Such is his love. He embraces his whole creation in the Cross, its ugliest and its weakest, in his most beautiful strength.

The whole of the Gospel is this: there is nothing in all creation that God has not redeemed and cannot redeem, for God is love. Look at the unlikely people Jesus included among his closest associates!

The Gospel is about dismantling the barriers that we sinners, disabled by sin, have set up between us and our fellow creatures. Those who enter on the work of the Kingdom must set aside their own prejudice and seek what God sees in all his creatures, the potential of grace. The God whose name is Love (1 John 4.16) seeks lovers who will extend their love to all his creatures.

When we welcome people with disabilities into our churches they will minister to us in ways beyond our present imagining, adding to the richness of the fellowship, bringing to worship a new dimension. Their simplicity approaches again the childlikeness without which none of us shall enter the kingdom of heaven (Matt. 18.1-4).

Power to transform lives

We live in an age that has run short of hope. We hear about lives traumatized by violence, poverty, or broken relationships, and are told they can never be fully restored. Abused children will grow up damaged. Long-term unemployment renders people incapable of work. To the clashes of nation, race and religion there seems no end. Do we Christians really believe in the power of God to change lives? We talk about new life in Christ, but how widely do we believe it is available?

Perhaps we may rekindle hope by looking at the effect of encountering God's love on people who are severely disabled. Here we see the power of the Word on the wordless, and the impact of divine love on those whom many do not find lovely.

'I call you by name', says the Lord, 'you are mine' (Isaiah 43.1). The Bible continually stresses the importance of names: people are carefully named and sometimes renamed. This resonates for those who work with those who have learning disabilties, for our friends love names. 'I'm John. What's your name?' may be almost the whole of a man's conversation. Often seen *en masse*, recognized more by condition than individuality, they constantly claim their own names and seek to identify others by name. 'You are rude, Mum', Richard observed. 'You just say "Good morning" to the station man. He has a name.' Travelling alone, he had soon discovered that this was David. My son greets those who serve him with, 'I'm Richard. What's your name?' and does not see why I find it harder to do the same.

One year he distributed invitations to a birthday barbecue to all at the special worship group. The mother of one friend, not herself a church-goer, was moved to tell the group's leader that in twenty-six years this was the first time her daughter had received a *personal invitation with her name on it*, not just a communal one to all at the special school or day centre. Here in the church group she was known by name! That mother later gladly attended her daughter's baptism as a believer, declaring that going to the church was 'the best thing that's ever happened' to her daughter.

Often it is Christian staff at care homes that first bring their people to church, but that young woman was brought to the group's second meeting by a man, with more severe learning disabilities, who was eager to share his delight in the new worship group. Those who had set up the group were amazed: he was one of those they wanted to serve: they had not thought of him as an evangelist.

Dancing in the Big Top

Gary and Teresa Knott took their children and two residents from a Shaftesbury residential home to SpringHarvest. Each morning they went to the Causeway meetings for people with learning disabilities and were encouraged. One evening they saw the power of God moving in Michael, a man with Down's Syndrome. They saw him enjoying himself and, at the same time, glorifying God as he danced to the music, alone or with a couple of professional Christian dancers, at the front of the Big Top before 5,000 people!

Later people were invited to come to the front to receive a special anointing from God by the laying on of hands. To his friends' surprise, Michael went forward. When they returned to their caravan, they asked him what had happened and, with his very limited vocabulary, Michael replied 'God!' and punched his fists to show how he had been touched by the living God.

They returned home convinced that they must help to develop Michael's new-found faith. Out of that experience and with the support of their local church, developed the work of the Harlow Causeway Group, the Living Stones Drama Group and the Michael

Roberts Charitable Trust which has become a considerable local force for the good of people with severe disabilities.

Some years later Michael was at a BUild conference in Sheffield. Much of the day he sat quietly, just enjoying the atmosphere but seeming a passive participant. After the final benediction, he rose and limped around the circle with a gracious gesture, a warm smile, and the words 'Thank you' for every person who had been responsible for some part of leading or organizing the day, including those 'behind the scenes' who easily go unnoticed. Michael had observed and appreciated all.

More changed lives

Frank was sixty when he left a big hospital for a group home in London and began to attend the local church. After a time he asked for believer's baptism. The minister tried to prepare him but did not think he understood much. Beset by doubts, that minister went to the church on the day appointed. Was he really about to baptize a believer? In trooped a dozen strangers. These proved to be Frank's relatives, coming because they had seen such a change in him over the past three months and wanted to know more about what lay behind this. With confidence renewed, the minister led Frank into the pool.

Thomas, a crotchety man of middle age, whose only conversation seemed to be complaint, was one of a group taken to morning worship at the local Baptist church. Hazel, who organized transport and befrienders, always found herself left to look after grousing Thomas in his wheelchair. As the weeks passed, Thomas grumbled less and smiled more. He began to turn to Hazel after the benediction each week, saying, 'Jesus really loves me, doesn't he? When Hazel visited his home, she had only to enter the room to see

Thomas' face light up with pleasure. Usually a 'backroom worker', Hazel surprised herself by wanting to tell a BUild conference about Thomas, who had died not long before. 'I don't know what I did to deserve it, but Thomas was my friend and I was his', she marvelled. For Thomas, Hazel had become the instrument of God's transforming love and peace. She had been, in the words of the hymn, 'as Christ to him'.

In most of those churches that have been running special groups focused on appropriate worship and teaching for people with learning disabilities there are probably examples of life-changing experience of God's love and affirmation of their worth. As I write, I 'hear' the girl delighted to repeat at a BUild conference her baptismal testimony - voiced not in words but by playing on a triangle 'O wonderful love'.

Pastoral Concerns

When a baby is born with evident disability, the parents will be glad of friends who share their shock and sorrow. It is never easy to express sympathy effectively and it is tempting to slip into well-meant phrases - 'They bring their love with them', 'Such children are always happy'. Parents try to smile politely but would rather just be told that others feel their agony.

Parents expect a normal baby, 'worth' all the effort of pregnancy and labour. When it is obvious that the child is severely impaired, it is a shock. There is a sense of bereavement, the loss of the anticipated child, coupled with anxiety about what they have to care for instead.

Some conditions are immediately recognized at birth, others only become apparent gradually, as development lags behind the norm. Parents may deliberately avoid seeing the signs - or they may worry over them and be jollied along by doctors and health visitors until none can avoid the diagnosis.

However the knowledge comes, it will be unwelcome and take time to assimilate. Being a Christian does not provide immunity from suffering or despair. Parents may well have questions. Is it something I have done? Can we cope? Do we want to? What will people think? How will it affect us? How will it affect our other children? They expect to care for a helpless new baby but worry more about anticipated future problems. The advice used to be, 'Put the child away and start again'. This option is no longer encouraged: usually Mum is left to cope.

All too often it is just the mother. It is well known that many fathers walk away from disability. Some mothers devote themselves so completely to the child with special needs that they have little energy left for other members of the family, even their other children.

This is both understandable and sad. The time and effort that necessarily goes into the daily care of a child with multiple disabilities is exhausting and long term. It is very hard to maintain anything like normal family life. Nevertheless, where families stay together and share the care, it is likely to be better for all members.

Greater skill in keeping premature babies alive carries the unfortunately greater risk of some surviving but with disabilities. The number of people in the population with intellectual impairment is rising. At the same time, antenatal testing for some disabling conditions, with the offer of abortion, has become common practice in Britain. From a grandmother's perspective, I am glad I had my babies in 'the old days'! Early pregnancy now seems overshadowed by the fear that the scan will reveal some abnormality and the need to consider abortion. My daughter-in-law tells me that there is now less *pressure* to abort, but that too was common a few years ago and one of her friends was faced with that. That couple rejected the risk of further tests for Down's Syndrome, since they would not abort life on religious grounds. Happily, their little girl was fine, but it had cast a miserable shadow over six months of the pregnancy.

I do not like the idea of abortion yet am also uneasy with the pro-life lobby. It is easy to be dogmatic about other people's lives and to enthuse about severely disabled children - if you do not have to care for them day in, day out. My own son's disabilities are not too severe, but they brought quite a lot of extra stress and effort and, for some years, a sharp sense of isolation from normal life. There are brain-damaged children who can do nothing for themselves except cry on and on, and tortured parents whose devoted care can achieve little improvement in their child's quality of life. Many families are broken by the strain of coping with disability at all levels of severity.

These very difficult areas cannot be treated fully here but they must be matters of pastoral concern. Consider, for instance, parents like that above, where an early check suggests their foetus may have Down's Syndrome or Spina Bifida. While awaiting further tests, they may decide to abort if the tentative diagnosis is confirmed. Happily the baby is normal so is left to develop in the womb. All goes well until the birth, when a difficult labour results in temporary but disastrous loss of oxygen to the brain. The baby is born more severely disabled than was likely with the predictable condition. Having taken that earlier decision to abort, how will they now adjust to their brain-damaged baby? That seems to me a much worse scenario than learning, as I did, that the lovable bundle already in my arms had Down's - and that was quite hard enough.

Pastorally, the advice can only be to let your imagination travel with the parents before you come out with conventional phrases. The friend who honestly admits she does not know what to say may be the one who helps most. Listen to the parents and answer *their* questions, even if those are not what you expect. If the parents are not actually asking *why* it happens, but rather what hope there is of ever sharing their faith with this child, that is probably the burning question for them - and is probably easier to answer!

Parents are likely to be and to remain over-sensitive about the child who is severely disabled. It helps when the church accepts and welcomes their baby, defuses their embarrassment, shares their anxiety and sets all this in a wider perspective.

The dedication service

The occasion when the baby known to have disabilities is presented to the church will be painful, whether in a church with infant baptism or in the Baptist way with the dedication of parents. Some families avoid this altogether. Some churches have refused it as having little meaning in such a case - a cruel rejection! In families where other babies would be solemnly but with rejoicing presented at church, it cannot be right or Christlike to neglect or refuse the one who is born disabled. A caring church will find ways to make the occasion appropriate and affirming.

As we offered God our limp baby, six weeks old, for whom so many doors had already been closed, my husband and I wondered about promising to 'teach him the truths and duties of the Christian faith'. We had by then accepted that no amount of prayer was going to take away the condition, so that promise felt a bit hollow when we doubted whether he would ever be able to understand. Thanksgiving was somewhat muted. We were greatly helped by sensing the church's commitment to share the responsibility with us. Nearly forty years on, the membership of the church has largely changed but the corporate commitment has never wavered. No wonder Richard loves Christ and his church!

We resisted joining one of the parents' support bodies (Mencap or the Down's Syndrome Association, which had recently been formed), feeling reluctant to take on board the pain of other disabled families. In the early days we could afford to avoid bodies that help many parents because we found our natural support group in the church. Later it seemed right to help others through BUild.

Sadly, not all families find the church so supportive. One family, wanting some Christian recognition of their son but refused a dedication service, resorted to the parish church whose vicar was more accepting. Moving some years later they settled into an apparently more welcoming Baptist church. There the minister judged the family well integrated within the fellowship, but the mother saw it differently. Going to worship was all right, but the family gradually dropped out of social occasions because they found their son was not really accepted among other children. 'It felt awkward ...Evasion is much harder to cope with than honesty, and far more exhausting, but we have got the message now ... it is simply that they cannot understand the problems and I do not know the answers.' Pain accumulates and each bad experience makes it harder to try again.

As children grow up, inclusion in all appropriate activities becomes part of pastoral care. What is appropriate will vary and the disabled child may well need a special helper, but the child and the family will benefit from a church willing to try.

Programmes of intensive early stimulation are now seen to improve the development of many disabled children. Mothers are eager to undertake anything that will help their child achieve as much as possible, believing this will give better quality of life. Friends need to understand how demanding such programmes can be, especially when rewards are slow to appear, and how parents can feel guilty for failing to give more time. Parents may need sympathetic help, both with the programmes and in maintaining a sense of balance. This is important for the sake of their other children, for their own well-being, and for that of the disabled child. If the parental expectations are too high for too long it can lead to the child becoming conscious of constantly being a disappointment to loving, praying, hopeful parents. Pastors and friends need to realize that there are some very sensitive balances here.

Christlike care

'Sir', they said to the disciple, 'we would see Jesus' (John 12.21). It is not often that someone says that to us, but many are potentially interested in religion and have big questions about the meaning of life. They are often quick to criticize Christians but, when they see in us some evidence of special, Christlike qualities, they are more likely to ask what makes us tick. When Christians are seen to give some of their precious time to help run the special group, or to look after a child with challenging behaviour to give the mother a break, others become aware of the motivating faith. If we let Christ dwell in us richly, we shall find ourselves undertaking things no selfish instinct would ever prompt - and others may catch a glimpse of Christ's glory.

A child of six with learning disabilities and epilepsy, usually pleasant and teachable, was liable without warning to become horrifyingly violent. 'It's as though a switch is flicked in her brain and she becomes a different person'. The father had deserted, the mother's relatives were kind to the older sister, taking her out for treats whose happiness the poor mother missed while she trailed around special schools and clinics trying to get help for her little one. 'This church is the only *normal* place I can go with my child', she told me.

There six church members had arranged a rota, taking turns to look after the little girl at church and to provide someone 'on call' if the mother needed help during the week. One of these, a retired professional man, had had to restrain the child when she had 'flipped' at the holiday club the previous week. He had a big wound across the temple as a result. Nevertheless, he was back, taking his turn, being 'as Christ' to that child and her mother, for whom there was healing in his wounds. In such ways is the Word made flesh today.

Respite provision

There is rarely enough respite provision, either of residential care or of willing 'sitters' to give parents an evening off duty. Churches can help. Individual friends can learn about particular care needs and win the mother's trust: it is no good having an evening out if you worry all through it!

One church decided to make a big effort to give disabled children a happy day and parents a break, perhaps a relaxed shopping trip or a chance to take their other children out, on one Saturday each quarter. Another church supported members trying to set up good respite care for profoundly disabled children.

The more complex the disabilities, the harder it is to find appropriate provision. One mother could find a home for autistic adults, a home for those with epilepsy, another for those with cerebral palsy, but none would take her daughter who had all three.

Growing up

The adult with learning disabilities faces questions about housing, work, and level of independence. A pastoral ear, ready to listen and clarify the pros and cons, may help those who have to take decisions. Young people need encouragement as they branch out and value friends who take an interest in their new experiences. If they are disabled that need is even greater. Parents also need sympathy and reassurance as they let go, especially when they have long had to be over-protective. This can be a huge challenge and is not always faced up to.

Adults also become more aware of the way the world views disability and that can be painful for them. Those who have physical disabilities but good brains often protest loudly about attitudes towards them. Those with learning disabilities are less articulate but are often aware that people like them are devalued in society. As a 'Down's mother', I wonder sometimes about news items concerning those with Down's Syndrome. An Oxford student abducted and murdered was a big story a few years ago, while the same thing happening to a Down's girl around the same time was a minor one.

A Down's baby is made a ward of court because parents resist life-saving surgery, and current affairs programmes wheel on mothers with their Down's toddlers to say how much they love their babies yet they wish they had known to abort them. Does it never occur to TV news teams that their regular audiences include a goodly number of adults, like Richard, who have the condition and can understand much of this discussion? I happened to be with Richard, a lover of the 'soaps', when *East Enders* showed a young mother standing by her Down's baby's cot, holding a pillow. Mercifully she resisted the temptation. Been there, done that, I thought as I tried to help Richard understand the mother's distress.

Many people, learning disabilities notwithstanding, are capable of taking mature decisions for themselves, but friends may help them think things through. Some will form special friendships, perhaps leading to marriage. A disabled couple contemplating marriage talked to a good friend. They grasped that marriage involved long-term commitment. They needed help with paperwork and planning. They did not appreciate church friends who assumed they did not know what they were doing, and who suggested it was 'unwise', or even that they should find 'some alternative'! They objected that other couples would not have such extra hurdles put in their path.

Another woman seriously considered a proposal, asking, 'Is this was God intends for me?' She concluded it was not, although 'it would have been so much easier to be married'. 'Why?' asked her friend. 'When my father goes, there is no one', came the sober reply, 'but I know God will take care of me.'

Love and care can be expressed in many simple, everyday ways, like remembering to send birthday cards to those who probably receive little personal post. Many adults with learning disabilities love birthdays: as children, they valued days when they felt special and important, and they retain a childlike delight in celebration. Friends do well to recognize this. Bake a cake, present a gift in pretty wrapping, make them feel 'special' in a good way.

Six ways to welcome people with learning disabilities to your church

Most of this advice comes from Joan Riley, and the following section on communication from Pat Maisch, both of whom have much experience of work with people who have severe disabilities in and out of the church. Joan was long involved with a special church group with the pleasing acronym CAMEO - 'come and meet each other'. Pat has led a large church group for people with a wide range of disabilities, while her professional work has been with those with severe disabilities.

1 **Smile**: everyone likes to be greeted with a smile and a handshake.

2 **Talk** to the person. Remember that many people only 'pick up' one, two or three words from a sentence. So if you say, 'Go and get a spoon from the kitchen, find a sugar bowl, and put more sugar and the spoon in it', the person with a learning disability may get a spoon but not know what to do next. Equally you may find a someone who can carry out the whole task unaided and maybe bring the biscuits as well. My son cannot grasp a spoken list of items but will work systematically down a written list. Experiment with what helps because success is good for the morale.

   You may not be able to understand everything that is said to you. Ask the person to repeat - most are patient about this. If you still do not understand, engage the assistance of the parent or carer, or even a friend who also has learning disabilities (such friends are often good interpreters). Do not be alarmed if the person seems to have great difficulty in getting words out; allow time for speech to come. 'Brian has a lot to talk about but he talks slowly', Richard explains of one of his friends. 'He always has lots inside his mind.'

During hymns and songs, many people with learning difficulties sing their own words. Often they respond to the rise and fall of the music very well, and their singing is no more distracting than someone singing 'in tongues'. Others may find it easier to join in by signing the ideas in the hymn or just putting appropriate actions to the words. That can be encouraged as a way to help people join in.

3   **Learn some sign language.** Makaton signs, simplified from British Sign Language used by the deaf, are the kind most often used to reinforce speech for those with learning disabilities. Local Day Centres may run short courses, or be willing to arrange this for a church. The Makaton Charity (Manor House, 46 London Road, Blackwater, Camberley GU17 OAA - info@makaton.org) also offers materials, including DVD, to help people learn to sign, word lists, and some prepared materials, e.g. the Lord's Prayer, the Christmas story. Christmas carols.

4   **Transport:** If there are people with learning disabilities living near the church, whether with family or in a group home or hostel, consider offering transport to and from the church. Often that is the only way they will be able to attend services and social functions. Some homes have no vehicles, or a shortage of drivers. Insurance will need to be checked, but transport to anything is often a problem and might be a good point of contact if a church wants to help with local needs. Invitations with transport to a harvest supper or some other church party may be a good way to make initial contact.

5   **Include people in activities**: coffee mornings, women's groups, men's groups, house groups - as well as times for worship. Do not worry too much about whether they will understand the talking part: if the meeting has a friendly atmosphere and they feel part of that, they will probably enjoy being included. Try to ensure there is one particular befriender beside each person with a learning disability, ready to guide them through, at least until they get the hang of the meetings.

Many would love to be asked to help. Some are good at greeting people, some give out hymn books or news sheets, gather the offering, stuff envelopes. Some are able to take a turn in reading scripture. Many will join in a time of open prayer. Some people with learning disabilities have lovely singing voices. Some really enjoy helping to tidy up at the end of a service or meeting. Give them a chance to contribute in whatever way they can.

Remember that they may learn slowly but once they understand what to do many are conscientious, reliable workers.

6   **Set up regular meetings** for people with learning disabilities. A number of churches now offer a meeting, some primarily social but most offering Christian teaching and worship geared to their special needs. Some do this weekly, some fortnightly or monthly - the frequency will depend mainly on the available helpers. The meeting may be a co-operative venture with Christian parents, day care or residential workers; it will need their backing, even when organized and staffed by the church. Sometimes it may be an ecumenical effort with two or more local churches involved.

A worship meeting should be fairly relaxed yet semi-formal with a drink and biscuit, some songs, a short story told in simple words, perhaps using pictures or drama, and time for people to contribute their own prayers or to name someone for whom they want to pray. Sharing news can be a helpful way to lead into prayer.

Some churches simply make premises available to an outside group, but that can help break down barriers and begin to make contacts. Churches that have attended to disability access often now have attractive premises for those seeking venues.

Whatever the way a church gets involved, members should be aware that they are dealing with vulnerable adults. The Baptist Union has a helpful pack, *Safe to Belong*, offering guidance on this.

Churches wanting to welcome people from local group homes should be aware that these vary a lot in ethos. Some, like L'Arche communities, have a strong sense of corporate activity and invitations to all, disabled and staff members, would be appropriate. Other homes, keen to encourage individuality and wary of group activity, respond better to approaches to one person at a time. It would be appropriate for someone to call with an invitation to the Harvest Supper or Carol Service for anyone who might be interested as long as they realize the need to follow this up with transport and introductions. Such homes may welcome volunteers willing to befriend individual residents and take them out shopping etc. Some positively welcome church links, others will not be interested - just like the rest of the population.

Sometimes it proves possible for a church to arrange a Christian group meeting as an optional activity at a Day Centre or local group home. If clients or residents are found to like it, staff are likely to co-operate. Those who enjoy such a group will probably bring friends. Such a group may be deliberately for worship or have a more social context, but either way it can be a time for sharing joys and concerns and include prayer. Creative work may well be enjoyed. Some people are able to express their feelings better through art, or simply enjoy making things.

The Local Disability Team would be able to advise and effect introductions, if the church does not already have contacts. They are usually delighted if people want to include their clients.

When the BUild work began, it was not unusual to meet wariness and even resistance to anything to do with church among the staff of residential homes and bodies like Mencap. I remember one church worker lamenting that, after a change of staff, a man who liked attending the morning service found his bath-time had been changed to 10.30 Sunday morning. Since those days there has been a considerable change of attitude. It is a cause that the secular body, the Foundation for Learning Disabilities, has taken up with some vigour at an inter-faith level. It is now widely recognized that spirituality is a proper human right and that this applies to people with learning disabilities. John Swinton, now a leading academic in the area of learning disability with a background in specialist nursing, defines spirituality as the human quest for 'meaning, purpose, self-transcending knowledge, meaningful relationships, love and commitment, as well as the sense of the Holy amongst us.' If people who have disabilities wish to go to a place of worship, the care staff should make that possible. How willingly and regularly this is done will still depend on how well the church - or other place of religious worship - makes them welcome.

Communication

Most people with learning disabilities have communication problems, but the range is wide. Some have no speech. Others can hold a good conversation on something they really know about (my son's area of special knowledge is hymnody and he constantly amazes everyone with the way he can locate a hymn from a middle line or find an appropriate hymn or song to fit any given theme). Most fall in between the extremes and value conversation at a suitable level. Caring friends can help in various ways.

As a general rule, make eye contact to help hold attention and take care to speak clearly, in a suitable tone of voice, using easily understood words. Where appropriate reinforce words with gestures and facial expressions. Saying 'no' with a sweet smile does not help someone to understand, whereas a solemn shake of the head may get the message across. Be comfortable with silence and allow people to respond in their own time. Do not talk down to disabled people. Avoid treating adults like children or children with disabilities like babies.

Eye contact is too challenging for some people, especially those with autism. With them it may be better to shift the focus elsewhere, perhaps to what is engaging their attention.

Where people have very little language, help them use what they have by careful phrasing. If you ask questions they can answer with a simple 'yes' or 'no', that will involve them in the conversation. A succession of people coming to exchange names and shake hands may make all the difference to feeling part of a gathering rather than an outsider.

Now that Makaton is widely used, it helps if some church friends make the effort to use it. Not everyone with a learning disability is able to use it. Some have private signs, known perhaps only in the family: get help from parents or carers so that you recognize these, especially those for basic needs like wanting a drink or the toilet.

Often those with limited speech will keep repeating a familiar word or phrase, or echo what is said to them. Some give up on speech because no-one bothers to listen. Some can sing words clearly although unable to speak them. Garbled speech is often clearer sung, and sometimes it is possible to have sung dialogue where speech gets no response.

Different conditions may respond to different approaches. Many Down's people have an instinct for acting and may use that to communicate. People with autism may respond best to simple language spoken in a soft voice, perhaps finding signs more comfortable than speech, and need plenty of time and space to respond. Where there is visual impairment, it usually helps if you speak before touching to warn of your approach. The terrors experienced by one deaf-blind man with profound learning disabilities were much reduced when a therapist realized he could be given tactile clues: a mug to feel before meals, a sponge to indicate bath-time, etc. This gave him a chance to anticipate what was happening next.

So be ready to use gestures, assorted vocal sounds, facial expression, and things to touch as aids to communication.

Bereavement Care

Audrey Saunders, a Cruse bereavement counsellor, had to help her sister cope with the loss of parents. Her own experience was backed by other studies, especially a course on 'Death and Dying' led by Dr Lester Sireling at St George's Hospital, Tooting, in 1995. The Baptist Union enabled her to attend this on behalf of BUild. She offers thoughtful advice.

The one certainty in life is death and people with learning disabilities have to face the pain of loss and go through the same process of grief as everyone else. Intellectual and emotional maturity are different and some are mature emotionally, having learned to cope with extra difficulties, which may include deafness, impaired vision, speech difficulties, epilepsy, heart disease, and other chronic conditions which often occur in conjunction with intellectual impairment.

We are all affected by death and loss. Why should we expect people with learning disabilities to be any different? Yet many hopefully assume that they will not notice the loss, so ignore their real feelings. Sadly they are not always given the opportunity to grieve and may even be surrounded by a conspiracy of silence. If the bereavement means that they need to move into residential care for the first time, this will contribute to their feelings of insecurity and fear.

Normal grief is expressed in a variety of ways, mental and physical. Bewilderment and disbelief mingle with shock, anger and guilt. It is not unusual to feel angry towards the person who has died. Eventually, over a period of many months, there will be a gradual acceptance of the loss, although memories triggered by a piece of music, a once favourite perfume or aftershave can send the sufferer back to square one. Grieving is a long process.

Sometimes a person will become 'stuck' and the grief will become chronic. Worse still, the person will become seriously depressed. When this happens, expert help is needed. If the bereaved person has a learning disability, diagnosing depression will be more difficult. It may be that what the family or carer will notice is a change of behaviour, such as a refusal to go to the training centre, a loss of appetite, a general restlessness and anxiety, or even aggressiveness.

It is even more difficult when there is no verbal communication. Maureen Oswin, in her leaflet *The Right to Grieve* (1981), tells how one lady, very disabled, nearly starved to death when admitted to hospital after her mother died. She eventually found comfort in the ward kitchen, sucking pieces of Marmite toast. The staff thought she had probably spent many hours in the kitchen with her mother.

Sheila Hollins and Lester Sireling produced a number of 'Books Beyond Words' to help people with severe learning disabilities cope with difficult aspects of life. These include *When Mum Died* and *When Dad Died*, which could be very useful to anyone wanting to help such people cope with bereavement (available from Amazon).

Death of an adult child with learning disabilities

The death of a child before the parent is always distressing: it is the wrong order. But the death of a son or daughter who has learning disabilities may also be welcomed by the parents, especially if they have anxieties about who will care for their child when they are no longer there. Parents have a very deep anxiety about this. The grieving parent may even admit to sometimes having wanted to kill the child. All this creates its own painful sense of guilt. We are appalled when we hear of a father, on losing his wife, drive himself and his son into deep water to drown, but really it is all too understandable. Those ministering to the parents should try to grasp how they feel. They will most help the parents if they accept the reality of such shocking feelings, but draw attention to all the care and love that has been given to that child, sometimes over many years.

Other parents may feel that they have failed in their care. They may be very angry with anyone who says that it was 'for the best' - 'Was this child only fit to die?' The family will have experienced multiple losses over theyears, starting with grief for the child they expected but never had. This grief will have been renewed many times at the various missed or delayed milestones of normal childhood development. The degree of disability is immaterial to the intensity of the grief.

This long process will have affected other members of the family, not just the parents. Siblings especially need to be reassured that it is all right for them to continue with their lives. Their feelings too may vary between relief and guilt - relief that a possible future responsibility has been avoided, and guilt that they feel relieved. They need to know that it is normal to feel like this and to be reminded of the good things in the relationship.

Occasionally parents may so sanctify the memory of the child who has died that siblings are left feeling totally inadequate. If this happens, both the parents and the siblings may need a good deal of help.

Death of a parent

This is the second most common cause of people seeking bereavement help from Cruse. People with learning disabilities too will be affected by the death of a parent. Such a son or daughter may have depended heavily on the parent who has died. That parent may also have clung to the child and been over-protective, especially if a lone or lonely parent coped with a great deal of stress on his or her own. The son or daughter may always have been regarded as special - 'Daddy's girl'. Dependence on a surviving parent is likely to be both physical and emotional.

It is not unusual for a bereaved person to feel panicky, and the person who is both disabled and bereaved may need much encouragement to go back to the training centre or youth club. Friends can help by gentle encouragement and by taking an interest in what is happening, especially on open days or other special occasions.

Then there are the needs of the siblings who may be expected to take over the role of main carer. In addition to their own grief, they may be afraid of their new responsibilities and feel guilty about this.

At the death of a parent, difficult decisions may need to be made regarding the future of the son or daughter who is disabled. Some form of residential care may be the answer. The family will need friends and advisers willing to be alongside them, to listen, affirm and support their decision.

The funeral

This is the time for the final farewell. How this is done will vary according to family beliefs and traditions, but it is important to include the member with learning disabilities. If the family is going to visit the chapel of rest, he or she may find it helpful to have something specific to do: to light a candle, or take a farewell card or picture to place on the coffin. Enlist the help of the funeral director who may have other suggestions about providing a positive memory.

During the actual committal, ensure that someone helps the disabled person to take part. Even a severely disabled person may feel part of the proceedings if given a hug.

Death of someone in a group home

Many people with learning disabilities now live in group homes or special units. It is very important that they are allowed to grieve when a fellow member of their group dies. The familiar person who always sat there for tea will be missed, and adjustments will need to be made when a new resident joins the family.

Some may be frightened that they too are about to die, or they may appear to accept the death very casually - 'That's another one gone'. Either way, it is important that they are allowed to take part in the final farewell if they wish to do so. Enlist the help of the funeral director, and perhaps plant a shrub or rose-bush later as a memorial. One resident insisted that his ashes should be scattered around the group home where he had lived: the chaplaincy made sure that this happened.

Remember that carers grieve too and need support.

Carers also move on to new jobs and people in group homes have to get used to new people with new ways of doing things. There can be a measure of bereavement in that situation. Compare such changes with those that take place in any job when a new boss arrivs and you will understand better the difficulties that may arise.

How to help

• Be there and listen. Use familiar words and signs when speaking. Mention the dead person by name.

• Look at photographs, if appropriate. Share pleasant memories.

- Take some favourite food or scented flowers. If it is not possible to communicate by words, it may be possible by smell, by touch and by holding.

- Help to open the window on the world again, and help the bereaved to smile and laugh again.

- If you have someone with learning disabilities in your church or living nearby, take time to get to know them and their family. When there is a bereavement, the comfort of known friends will be most easily accepted.

- Remember the needs of other members of the family, and affirm and support difficult decisions they may have to make.

Normalization

Siôr Coleman, former BUild secretary with long experience as a chaplain in the South Birmingham Mental Health (NHS) Trust, explains some of the principles of normalization and advocacy.

Much work among professionals in the field of learning disability has been fired by a philosophy known as 'normalization' or 'social role valorization'. In a world struggling with jargon, this seems to contain a lot of it, but beyond the jargon is much commonsense. The heart of normalization is that it encourages in professionals a particular *attitude of mind*. It is less concerned with *what* is done than with *how* it is done.

The questions to ask run like this. Would I want this done to me or my friend? Do I like the idea of living in a residential setting and sharing a bedroom with more than three others? Do I value the right to choose my own clothes? Do I value the right to go to church? Do I value the right to refuse to go to church? People with learning disabilities have often not enjoyed the chance to do or experience things which others take for granted. Normalization asks why anyone should be treated differently, believing that everyone has a right to have what they value respected by others.

Three main areas of concern are raised. The examples do not simply show what can happen but also reveal the underlying attitudes.

Integration and participation v. isolation

Isolation can happen when people are given accommodation which takes them away from the places and the people they know and therefore value. It may also happen in a church when a group of people with learning disabilities are welcomed but then end up sitting together, effectively isolated from most of the congregation. Isolation may occur when such people are transported in 'hospital buses' (sometimes emblazoned with 'A gift from...'), which mark them out and so isolate them even when they are going to a community-based event, like a session at the local bowling rink.

Enhancement of dignity and respect v. dehumanization

Dehumanization can happen when, for example, toilet and washing arrangements do not guarantee privacy, or when physical needs, like the provision of a ramp, are ignored because 'there are enough strong people to lift you up these steps' (reinforcing dependency). Do people with learning disabilities who are part of a worshipping congregation have the right to share in decision-making processes or are decisions made on their behalf? 'I'm sure they'd like to go on an outing together ...'

Use of language may also dehumanize. Defining people in terms of their condition or need, rather than their individuality, is a denial of their humanity. Generalizing statements, however well meant, often reveal an unfortunate attitude.

Age appropriateness

This is another area addressed by normalization. A person with learning disabilities may be classified by 'mental age'. What does that mean? Development is not necessarily even across the board. Thus one person might have a very low reading age, yet have much better road sense than a six-year-old child whose reading is quite advanced. Adults are not the same as children, even if they function at a 'childlike' level in some respects. They have more experience of life and are not helped by being treated like children. Inappropriate behaviour, especially in a social setting, may need to be checked, but saying 'naughty' as if to an errant child is unlikely to help.

The positive side

Normalization can appear to be very negative because it challenges commonly held assumptions which are not easily dislodged. Really, however, it is positive, human and accords with Christian understanding. Before God, everyone is special, valued and loved. We all need support at some time. Normalization is a signpost rather than a clearly defined map, but it points in the right direction.

> So
> - give people the opportunity to belong
> - treat them as individuals
> - encourage them to express personal choice
> - allow them to entertain as well as be entertained
> - enable them to join in conversations rather than be on the receiving end of an interrogation.

Such good practice helps those with special needs to enjoy things we like to think of as normal.

Advocacy

Advocacy - or Citizen Advocacy - is concerned with ensuring that everyone enjoys their rights as citizens, full members of their community. Some will require support to protect these rights. Those less able to speak for themselves need more articulate advocates. This is still a developing area, with much encouragement of self-advocacy and peer advocacy by people with disabilities on behalf of their fellows.

The advocate will need to partner the person to be represented and develop a relationship to understand the partner's particular needs. When necessary, the advocate will vigorously represent the partner's interests as if their own. Examples from one Advocacy scheme included a partner unhappy about the way his clothes were chosen. His advocate suggested changes to ensure his personal choices were heard and respected. Another partner lost some speech therapy support and the advocate got this restored.

Some people need long-term assistance of this kind, others may only need it through a crisis period. It may be particularly helpful at times of change, as when someone is being resettled into a new home.

There are various advocacy schemes around the country. Individual Christians and churches might consider becoming involved in various ways.

- Find out about local advocacy groups. Local social services or day care centres should be able to provide information.

- Consider training as an advocate. Some groups, working on limited budgets, might be grateful to use church premises for a series of training sessions for those interested.

- There may be people who need advocacy already in the church. Churches that have become sensitive to the issues raised by learning disability often provide good support of this nature, but might still appreciate help to strengthen this further.

- Talk to local chaplains. In addition to advocacy, there are other ways in which volunteers may provide quality support and friendship.

The Church's Open Door

In this section we look particularly at examples of good inclusive practice, the ways churches have found to reach out to and involve people who have learning disabilities.

Befriending

Fellowship and friendship are an integral part of church life. We are bound together in Christ and ought to be good at extending Christian love to people on the margins and at drawing them into the community. It is easier said than done, but many churches are actually quite good at it. Worrying about how to hold a conversation with those who find speech difficult will not be a great help, so try drawing them in to other activities. Steer them to the refreshments. Include them when showing the photos of last week's wedding or outing. Look for practical jobs they might help with. Many find that contributing in some way gives real assurance that they belong to the church. Most churches have plenty of simple, practical, regular jobs to be done - like putting up hymn numbers, tidying up after a service, filling envelopes with a circular letter, etc. Abilities vary and it may take time to learn what is required, but many become valued workers and thus share in the joy of Christian service.

Through a community scheme in Bristol, *Choices for Learning,* which helped people do things that really interested them, one woman who wanted to worship God was linked with a local church. In due course she joined the choir. Her enjoyment of music helped her join in other community activities, like going to local concerts and the theatre.

Provide work experience

Some churches go further and make opportunities for training and even employment available to local people with disabilities. They make links with day centres and give people a chance to help with lunches for the elderly, or with the mums and toddlers group, at the toy library, or in the church garden. It can be very difficult to find work experience for those who take time to learn a new task and work fairly slowly, especially in a society which assesses everything on a scale of profitability. When local councils ran both day centres and local park services, there was some incentive to employ the abler bodied as gardening assistants. That ended when councils began to subcontract gardening to firms who just had an eye on profit. The church, having different values and motivation, can be more patient and open about letting people with disabilities give, not just receive.

Remember that learning may be slow. My son took a whole summer learning to mow the lawn without cutting the cable to the lawnmower. I would soon have given up but his father has more patience. An earth trip meant that Richard could practice without risk of electrocution, but the cable acquired many joins carefully covered in insulating tape. Then suddenly Richard got the hang of it. For many years now his parents have rejoiced to be spared that chore, the lawn has been kept under control, and the replacement cable has not needed running repairs. It was worth that summer's effort.

Integrate or make special provision?

In recent years more churches have run special groups for children or adults with disabilities, and especially for those with learning disabilities. The emphasis may be on worship and teaching, or it may be social, or both - but all are about showing the love of Christ and that is rarely a one-way process.

Churches often ask whether it is right to have separate activities or should the focus all be on mainstreaming. The ideal is surely not 'either ... or' but 'both ... and'. Where people can join in regular activities, that is great. Young people who cannot read may swim well, play a respectable game of snooker, enjoy dancing or a country walk. Older people may enjoy the fellowship of a more formal meeting, even if they do not understand every word. A wide range of people share in churches' main worship services on Sundays.

Dedicated groups are not about separation but about special provision for those with special needs. Worship and teaching groups are more accessible for those who find learning difficult. They may indeed take part in the church's main worship sessions, but the teaching there will often fail to reach them. In their own group and at their own pace they will learn more about God and about worship, and this will enhance their participation in the integrated service.

Any philosophical doubts about special groups collapse when one sees them in action. They are so much enjoyed by *all* involved. The ready participation of members in song and prayer is a delight. In that context it does not matter if some enthusiastic voices are far from tuneful or if the words of some fervent prayers are only understood by God. Here people who may quietly conform in the main church worship - and others who may not fit in so easily there - are free to be themselves. Leaders find the ministry is never one-sided. When I visit such groups I always come away with a sense of missionary zeal to urge more churches to set them up. There must be a need for one in every district. Such groups readily serve people from several Christian traditions, for they deal in the basics of the faith we hold in common.

Special groups

Susan Wright has been involved in groups in three Baptist churches, in Edinburgh, Kent and Somerset. Although geographically far apart, there have been many similarities, not least the initial questions asked by members of the local church, the reticence and hesitancy of would-be helpers, and the commitment and hard work of everyone involved.

A group usually begins with the enthusiasm and concern of one church member who recognizes an unmet need and is challenged to do something about it within the fellowship. In Edinburgh, when the Ark Housing Association opened its first house for people with learning disabilities near Morningside Baptist Church, some of the residents came regularly to church. Susan remembers:

> They were welcomed and enjoyed the worship, but three of us in particular wondered how much of the 'teaching' content of the service met their spiritual needs. And so it was that our Special Bible Class /Study Group came into being. Of the three helpers involved at the beginning, two of us were already serving on the local residents' committee and therefore knew most of the people who came to the group. Most importantly of all, we enjoyed working with people!
>
> The Bible Class ran for many years, providing a place where Christian teaching was given in a small group. The meeting provided a time of worship, in singing, sharing of news, prayer, Christian teaching, and care and concern. Bible teaching material for adults with learning disabilities was sparse at this time and so material was adapted from other sources. Today material is more readily available to be

used or adapted to meet the needs of a particular group, so maybe the task is less daunting for those contemplating beginning a similar group in a local church.

The Kent group began with the enthusiasm of a church member who gathered others around him to set up a club for children and young people with learning disabilities, to provide a place where they could meet socially and enjoy themselves, and to give parents or carers a couple of hours respite. A small band of committed helpers (aged 16 to 70+) brought their own particular gifts and talents. All had the ability to get alongside the young people who came and show them love and friendship in the name of Jesus.

No special qualifications are needed to set up a church group for people with learning disabilities but the ability to get on with people is vital. Now that many more churches find that people with learning disabilities are worshipping with them, members are being challenged to look at their church programmes and activities and see if those who come amongst us are being welcomed and integrated into the Body of Christ, the Church. This may be a challenge to many of us, but it is one which we should endeavour to meet, 'the Lord being our helper'.

Reflections of a volunteer helper

John Harden described his feelings about helping at this club:

In the summer of 1991 a request for volunteers to help run a club for handicapped people was issued at Tonbridge Baptist Church. The Lord spoke to me clearly and told me I should help, which I volunteered to do. I had previously had no involvement with handicapped people of any description. Like most people, I thought of them as someone else's problem and I must admit I had serious reservations as to what I had let myself in for.

On that first evening I made a surprising discovery. Apart from their handicaps they were not much different from my own children. They had the same likes and dislikes, had similar needs and enjoyed the same games as other children. They were perhaps more demanding than children I had been used to, but their display of affection, to one another and their helpers, was and is quite remarkable.

Five years on I am still involved and glad to be so. It has been a pleasure to watch some of the younger ones grow up and develop and I never cease to be amazed at the things some of them are capable of.

It is not only the handicapped members that have changed in this period - it has been one of the best things to happen to me. My feelings for and understanding of the handicapped have changed completely. Those that only look on from the outside can have no understanding of what an uplifting and at times humbling experience being with these youngsters can be. I can only thank God that he brought me into contact with them.

The Welcome Club, Burnham on Crouch

Jackie Colgrove and her friend, Heather Trundle, went to an early BUild conference in Loughborough because they had persuaded their minister to hold a special 'Mencap Service' and he asked them to find out how to go about it. They probably received more encouragement than detailed advice, but soon after they began the Welcome Club which was soon drawing some twenty people with ages ranging from eleven to sixty.

They knew they first had to win the confidence of both these people and of their carers. They also had to persuade the church that this was a proper and significant ministry.

The Welcome Club offered a social evening, enjoyed by those who came, and giving carers a regular short break. The church granted the use of the hall without payment, so they did not charge for the club. Valuing freedom of choice, they offered a range of activities: snooker, table tennis, darts, hairdressing models, tuck shop, etc., or people could just sit and chat. Many just valued *space*. They enjoyed sharing their news. It helped that Jackie herself had a son at the Day Centre, so she often knew about things they were struggling to share. Gradually the helpers' Makaton improved!

On church social evenings, like discos or the Harvest Fun Night with games like apple bobbing, they also invited people from the hostel twenty miles away, where many of the club members went for respite breaks. Such occasions helped in getting to know people better.

They established one clear club rule: nobody would go outside the door. They also had to discover individual basic needs - like who needed help with toileting. The first night one man's glasses fell down the lavatory - hardly an auspicious start! There was plenty of shared laughter.

Spiritually they adopted a 'dripping tap' approach. They did not want to overwhelm newcomers with religion. They prayed for these new friends but only gradually introduced prayer to the club. Then they offered an optional worship time in the church adjacent to the hall. The worship included music, news, singing, dancing, short Bible readings and a talk. Before long everyone was opting in and, although it is intended to last half an hour, it can go on and on as many add their prayers. They know that God hears all prayers, spoken or silent. They are honest and sincere - and some prayers are startling. One girl prayed about how she loved her boyfriend kissing her. Another prayed that her parents would stop arguing - in a Mencap Service with her mother present!

Soon the Club was involved in leading the summer Mencap Service and a midweek Carol Service. The church was always full for these as club members proved good at inviting their friends from around the town. One year the Carol Service theme was 'Caring for our neighbours' and the drama crew acted out the plight of the homeless , showing how the love of Jesus is shared through the nightly soup-and-rolls run. Another time Zacchaeus had a splendid tree, concealing his stepladder, and his mother welcomed Jesus to the home with a nice cup of tea. Videos of these services are circulated afterwards, going into many homes, far beyond the regular congregation.

They sought to make the club widely known, with notices in doctors' surgeries, clinics, social services and library, and also through Essex Mencap. The Welcome Club proved good for making the church known in their small town and the town proved generous too. Burnham Charities helped towards running costs, the Rotarians bought a set of musical instruments, while the church bought easy-to-read Bibles all round. One lady's annual gift was home-made cakes for the Christmas disco. Whenever the club plans anything, money seems to be provided.

Officially the club hours are 7.30 to 9.30 p.m., but they are flexible. Jackie and Heather reckoned to be there from 7 till 10, saying there was no point in providing respite that was not long enough for carers to go to the cinema.

The main problems they encountered were a dearth of younger helpers and finding enough transport. Apart from Jackie and Heather, *all* the original helpers were over eighty and needed transport themselves. These elderly volunteers did a wonderful job, but to expand activities they needed younger help too. Unfortunately almost the only young people who seemed drawn to the church had disabilities themselves. The leaders found they could not cope with under-14s unless they had enough help to run a section for younger folk in parallel. The leaders soon realized that some were ready for deeper Bible study but the church had nothing suitable on offer. Could they find someone able to lead special studies? Once they had begun on this work, it seemed to grow in all directions.

At the church's invitation we held a BUild conference there. In theory Burnham on Crouch is a daft place to hold a day conference, way out on the Essex coast, approached by a slow train or winding country roads. In fact, it was one of the best of our conferences, and one of the best attended with some eighty people making the tortuous journey, thanks to the enthusiasm generated within that church and their zeal to spread the word.

The joy of learning

In her home in Winchmore Hill, the late Ena Robertson ran a special house group. Over several years her friends' biblical knowledge increased markedly. As they remembered the stories and made connections for themselves, Ena was able to use a wider range of scripture. They played a game in which she produced items to represent a Bible story - an apple for the Garden of Eden, a fish to remind them that Jesus called fishermen and that the fish is used as a sign of belonging to Jesus. Getting answers right is a real boost to confidence! They learned to distinguish easily the Christian aspects of Christmas from the 'Santa Claus stuff', where before it had all been muddled up. Learning new things took time, but once learned it was not forgotten.

On one occasion Ena took them to study the colourful banners in the church. One showed Pilgrim shedding his burden at the cross. The other, which she assumed would be harder for them, showed a globe surmounted by a crown. In fact, her group studied the latter and reasoned, 'That's the world. The thing on top looks like a crown. A king wears a crown. So it must mean Jesus is King of the world.' Turning to the other, all they saw was a poor man who had forgotten his shopping. Ena chuckled as she compared her own false assumptions with their grasp of her teaching.

Creative naming

These special groups are often exciting in their choice of names. While some are Causeway Groups, linked with Causeway Prospects, others to Faith and Light, and one or two have just adopted the BUild Club, we also have the Lifeway Bible Class, Welcome Group, God's Gang, Rainbow, Living Stones, Learning Together, Sunday Special, Kingfisher Club, Forward and Upward, New Beginnings Bible Group, Stepping Stones, Cross Links, Connect, Joy Class, and No Limits.

Some possible problems

In an early BUild survey, ministers envisaged various problems if, with the implementation of community care policies, groups of disabled people appeared at church. In practice, many churches have since had such groups join them and usually the churches have responded pretty well. Of course, there are occasional problems but Christian goodwill smooths most out.

A warm welcome goes a long way. For those not used to learning disabilties, the hardest part may be the first meeting. When nine people from the new hostel arrived at one church, the minister, a bit startled but with the right instincts, hugged them all, carer included - since it was not obvious which that was. That was in the 'good old days' before hugs were seen as suspect. There is a delicate balance to maintain when dealing with vulnerable adults. Friendly people with limited speech use their arms a lot in greeting and many have found the hardest part has been learning to accept their hugs and kisses. They will sadly get the message if people draw back and keep a 'safe distance'.

Interruptions and disturbance

Occasionally church members can be quite nasty about having disabled people around, complaining of disturbance etc., possibly with some reason. Such resistance to their presence may be understandable in society at large, but one might wonder about the nature of the gospel teaching when intolerance surfaces in a Christian church. At the same time, a time of peace and reverence is precious to many worshippers.

One church had quite a problem with a woman who was learning disabled and deaf. She could not speak but made sudden noises - loud enough to make the preacher jump. Some wanted to ban her, but it was clear that she got something from the service so others defended her right to attend. Gradually friends evolved a series of simple signs to guide her through the service. Her behaviour and attitude improved beyond all recognition.

Sometimes integration demands not only tolerance from other people but also a certain discipline for those who do not understand what is acceptable at a particular time or place. Many want to fit in but do not know how. Friends may need to give clear guidance to help them get it right. Where communication is limited, gentle hints are not much help. A firm approach is more likely to be understood, with plenty of demonstration and clear body language, not just words. A silencing finger on the lips may need to be backed with a frown, but then silence through the prayer should be rewarded with a warm smile of approval and perhaps the 'thumbs up' sign. Some people, disabled or not, may be naturally contrary, but it is unfair to assume someone will not co-operate when she has only been asked not to do something with courteous phrases and a kindly smile. That just fails to convey the message. As a mother, I know how often I have had to make myself look and sound sterner than I really felt if Richard was to learn. Not all will be able to learn 'suitable' behaviour but many will. Remember that helping people to behave appropriately may enable them to become happily part of the community where they want to belong.

Some churches are more easily disturbed than others. Some manage to delight in startling participation, like the church with a severely disabled little boy who always joins in the Lord's Prayer 'with much enthusiasm and shouting, to the delight and humbling of the congregation. The Lord loves it!'

Low incomes

Unfortunately most people with learning disabilities have to live on a low income and this affects participation. They are easily given too high expectations, perhaps mother used to afford coffee on every shopping trip, but alone her daughter must learn to forgo the little treat. Many have little sense of the value of money: a man may know his purse is heavy with coins but discover embarrassingly late that these do not amount to the price of a cup of tea. Church friends need to be alert to this, encouraging appropriate independence and quietly ensuring inclusion in events they would enjoy.

Shutting the world out

Sometimes people who are usually responsive seem to put up the shutters and their friends cannot get through to them. Many people with learning disabilities seem to have a peculiar ability to switch off from life around them. We all have 'off' days, but this ability to close down to the rest of the world can be disconcerting. Sometimes they are just too tired to cope with the effort of communication. Sometimes they have been upset, perhaps by something that happened earlier in the day but remains on the mind. Some suffer periodic bouts of depression: they are not, alas, immune from physical or mental illnesss.

The surprising thing is that so many with apparently so little going for them are cheerful and positive much of the time. One of Richard's friends used to be eager to tell everyone about his travels: equipped with his disabled pass, his hobby was to ride the London buses. He has a degenerative condition and within a few years became dependent on others to push him out in his wheelchair. But he is still a lovely man, always concerned for his friends, delighting in any outing or treat that comes his way.

Regular attendance?

A disappointment churches often mention is that people with disabilities from a group home will seem very keen, perhaps one or two will be baptized and join the church, and then suddenly they stop coming. Well, they are not the only ones! But when churches have tried hard to welcome such people, those who were close to them will wonder what they did wrong. They may have been upset by something said or done, but often their defection relates to staff changes at their home. Christian care workers may be keen to encourage residents to go to church, others do not normally go themselves but are pleased to see residents going out to something they like, others may be apathetic or positively anti-church and will not do much to help residents get ready in time. Church friends can help by getting to know the staff - and successive new staff, for they may change often. Sometimes when told that a resident no longer wishes to go to church, they may wonder how freely he has exercised his right of choice. With the right to spirituality more widely recognized these days, however, than in the early days of BUild, care workers are more likely to be helpful, even if only because it is another box to tick on the care plan.

Spiritual Matters

Recognizing faith

How do you evaluate another's faith? It is like being in love - when it happens, you *know*. When working with those who have learning disabilities, the question is more about how you recognize the knowing.

Faith often begins with the sense of being valued. A child with multiple disabilities and without speech entered the home of a loving Christian fostermother. Returning to hospital for yet more frightening treatment, he took his Children's Bible and clearly found comfort in the pictures, unerringly pointing out Jesus. The older boy in the next bed was so struck with this that he decided he had better try reading the Bible himself.

A miserable and timid young woman needed much patient support to settle into the special worship group, but eventually she could even manage a smile for visitors. Social workers reported that at the home she was now often heard singing instead of grizzling. They knew what had effected the change, because all her songs were of Christian nature, like 'Kum ba ya' and 'Alleluia'.

Another girl used to shuffle in and slump on a chair, her eyes on the floor, apparently unaware of her surroundings. An earlier traumatic experience had made her lose the speech she once had. People wondered why she came to the worship group at all, but gradually realized that something got through to her. She began to sit up straighter, to meet people's eyes with a lovely smile, and eventually even to whisper a word into the time of open prayer. When the worship group leader took a copy of the BUild version of the Lord's Prayer apart and put the pages up on the noticeboard, this silent girl was seen pointing to the pictures one by one and whispering the words!

The frightened comforted, the miserable made happy, the dumb beginning to speak - surely that has a Gospel ring! Those changes, though modest enough, bear witness to Christ's power to touch those who have very limited ability to learn. These are people who cannot read the Bible for themselves. They cannot understand much said by preacher or teacher. Their faith is probably limited to grasping that God loves them, disabilities and all, but they have encountered the love of God made flesh for them in the visible love and tangible care of Christian men and women. Through this means of grace God has touched their lives.

Healing issues

Where churches exercise healing ministry, a word of caution may be appropriate. Many find it hard to appreciate the difference between disease and disability, and this applies also to those with whom we are especially concerned here. When they see others healed of apparently lesser conditions, they ask why they cannot be changed too. Many a young person with Down's Syndrome must have prayed, like my teenage son, to be given 'a new face', implying all that would go with that. It is hard for parents to come to terms with the disability being part of the true nature of their son or daughter, and devastating to realize their child is not spared that hard realization. There is no space here to explore this - only to beg people to be alert and sensitive when this arises. It seems to be a fairly common problem for those new to faith. More mature disciples, even with learning disabilities, come to accept much that they do not understand.

Most people with disabilities pray readily for sick friends. In one group a popular member developed gangrene. Respecting bathroom privacy, the staff at his home missed the early signs. The group prayed that his legs would be made a normal shape and even the group leader thought he was recovering when the swelling went down, not understanding that this was a sign of deterioration as the leg wasted away. Eventually the leg had to be amputated. Cheerful as ever, he soon came to terms with a prosthetic leg, but his friends, no less than their house group leader, wrestled with the 'failure' of their prayers and with 'why did it happen to this lovely man?' Learning disability does not necessarily spare people the hard questions.

Believer's baptism

In the past it was often assumed that people with learning disabilities could not come to the kind of personal faith that Baptists look for, and that this did not matter because everyone knew that God loved them anyway. As a new parent, I found that profoundly unsatisfactory. At the very beginning of BUild's work I tackled the matter head-on at an area ministers' retreat. This was before we could see that Richard was capable of a faith of his own. Subsequently I had several ministers tell me of those who had repeatedly asked for baptism but their requests had not been taken seriously, assuming a lack of understanding. Challenged to think about this, they probed further when next approached and in each case the minister then realized this was a true believer, fit for baptism and possessing gifts for the enrichment of the church.

Appropriate preparation for baptism will vary according to the candidate's ability, but it often proves remarkably rewarding for all involved. Our minister found she sometimes struggled to find explanations Richard could grasp but he would tell her, 'Don't worry. It's all right!' Unlike most young people she had prepared, he brought no problems over virgin birth, miracles or resurrection. When they

came to prayer, praise and thanksgiving proved easy, but he found
'sorry' prayers hard: 'But I'm not bad!' Prayer for others was stimulating
as he found items from current news, as well as the needs of those
known to him. 'Prayer for ourselves' revealed some of his own inner
fears and sense of need for help. Richard is relatively able and could
follow a course simplified from that used with other young people.
He took particular delight in being given homework - an aspect of
normal teenage life of which he had evidently felt cheated until then!
For some, teaching has to be more constrained, perhaps focusing
mainly on the new beginning, with a birthday-like celebration with
cards and cake to help the candidate grasp the special importance
of the occasion.

I was at the baptism of another youth who had Down's
Syndrome and saw the shock on the face of minister and youth
worker as they entered the pool and realized the water had not been
warmed. The boy did not appear to notice how cold it was - clearly
his mind was on higher things, so thrilled was he to bear his witness
to Christ in the midst of his people. He had invited a number of
friends, including his class teacher from school, to witness this
important event - and that is typical of such disciples who are eager
to share their good news. Following Richard's baptism some of our
neighbours stopped me to ask me about believer's baptism. His
parents and elder brother are all more articulate than Richard, yet we
had not gone round like that, sharing our good news with everyone.

It is possible to make teaching simple yet not simplistic. The
BUild booklets were designed to help with baptismal preparation. I
remember the amazement of the ministers present when the three
lay women charged to prepare these told the BUild committee that
they intended to begin with the Trinity. We knew it was not an easy
doctrine but Father, Son and Holy Spirit are constantly spoken of in
church. It seemed important to offer something about each that they

could hold on to. So we looked at God the Father as creator, remembered the life, death and resurrection of Jesus, and thought of the Holy Spirit as the way we experience God's presence with us and helping us in daily life. Even if it is only possible to present a very few key concepts, these may prove life-enhancing.

Lord's Supper and Church Membership

When it comes to participation in the Lord's Supper and in the full life of the church, people often ask 'How much do they understand?' One is tempted to ask how fully any of us understand the mysteries of the faith, but the simple answer is that they will understand belonging and rejection. Certainly they should not be subject to *more* stringent tests than other people. Churches need to think about their understanding of the Gospel and of the church, and about their words of invitation to the Lord's table before they turn away someone who has learning disabilities but who wants to be part of that church. The drama of the Supper is possibly the most accessible part of Baptist worship for people who are not very verbal. That 'cup of blood' troubles some, but the association with Jesus, the sense of celebration and of the shared fellowship in communion are relatively easy to grasp. One minister wrote of a man with Down's Syndrome who was always at communion and received the bread with a loud 'Thank you very much, thank you!' It had become part of that church's liturgy and was appreciated by the rest of the congregation.

Paul Martin has written of a boy of twelve, severely impaired in both body and mind, non-verbal and responding little to stimulation, except in worship.

When I lift the loaf and proclaim the words of institution, 'This is my body given for you', it is a pleasure to see Craig's whole fragile and distorted body shake with joy and his face break into a wide grin. It is as if he intuitively knows that this is the high-point of worship'.

There are Baptist Christians who have learning disabilities who cherish church membership, recognizing it as a privilege and gladly undertaking regular responsibilities in a way that inspires their fellow members. My son loves Sundays and seizes on any opportunity to go to our church on other days and help with whatever needs doing. He is proud of his place on rotas for stewarding and serving food and drink. We delight in watching him swapping these duties, man to man, with the doctor and the train driver, the PhD student and the senior civil servant. He never seems more able than when he is active in the church. This is true for many others who have found fulfilment in their faith and in true belonging within Christ's church.

Discovering and releasing gifts

It is easy to assume that ministry will be one-sided, with much help and support given to people with disabilities. In practice, they have plenty to give in return. If you want to learn about the priesthood of all believers, try visiting a special worship group!

Often confident, competent people feel powerless when confronted by someone who is different, beyond their experience. With people who have learning disabilities they are disturbed because they do not know how to behave. That may be sad but it is natural enough. I am uncomfortably aware that, while I am usually at ease with Richard and his friends, among those with more severe conditions I still feel very awkward.

Often it is the sheer friendliness of many who have learning disabilities that breaks the ice. Many are caring, sensitive to other people and have a real gift for creating community wherever they go. Some are good at making people feel welcome, even if they cannot sustain long conversations, and may prove fine 'door-keepers in the house of the Lord'. Others enjoy serving refreshments and even washing up - it is so good to have a useful role.

Trevor Beeson, in *Window on Westminster* (SCM 1998, 2001) about life as a canon of the Abbey, writes of his additional role as Rector of St Margaret's, the church known for society weddings, a congregation 'drawn mainly from the political and professional classes', with an MP as churchwarden. The church was 'relaxed enough' also to encompass 'a number of unusual people', among them Enoch Hall, 'a simple man ... without the normal powers of reasoning and drive'. Enoch enjoyed worship, especially the music, and spent time at the church most days, always ready to perform any simple tasks.

He also enjoyed liturgical mishaps. If in the course of a service someone landed in the wrong place at the wrong time, whereas the rest of us would become uptight and cross at a failure of organization, Enoch would be greatly amused and fall about laughing. The failure was unimportant to him and I shall always be grateful for this insight into the mind of God which he shared with us.

So we have had a rather special person among us.

The voice of experience

One of the special groups that have proved good at discovering and drawing out the latent gifts of members is at Harlow. From experience in leading that Gary Knott and Paul Weldon had this advice to offer.

In many ways the discovery of gifts and skills in people with disabilities is achieved as it would be with anyone else. In other words, the opportunity to demonstrate ability and the giving of support and encouragement are likely to provide any church with a pool of people from all walks of life who are willing to use their gifts. The greatest step forward in this direction, with regard to people with disabilities, is the recognition that they are capable of possessing God-given gifts for use within the church. Once this often formidable barrier is understood and overcome, leaders will find themselves faced with the need to provide a forum in which these gifts can be discovered and used.

Most churches hold meetings throughout the week for particular groups: children, mums and tots, women's meetings, musicians ... the list goes on. It is often through these specialist groups, led by people who have a gift in that area, that gifts are first seen and nurtured. If it is possible, people with disabilities will benefit most, and display their hidden talents, in a group specifically catering to their needs. When we at Potter Street Baptist Church took on this challenge, providing a fortnightly meeting on a Wednesday evening, it was not long before we started seeing gifts in some of our members.

Practical points to bear in mind within such a group are those relevant in many similar situations:

- Give each member of the group time to settle and feel more confident.
- Encourage individuals to express themselves in a 'no threat' atmosphere.
- Allow everyone to contribute ideas and feel that they have a say within the group.
- Show respect for and value the thoughts and prayers of each person.
- Allow individuals freedom to praise and worship in their own way.

The last point, although easily agreed in theory, can be difficult in practice. It may be helpful to realize that people with learning disabilities often have far fewer inhibitions when praising the Lord. Churches where dancing, clapping, raising hands and other physical expressions of praise are not usually seen may find this disconcerting if they have an active and lively group like ours!

It may well be necessary to educate church members about disability. There have been many changes in the way we treat and care for people with all sorts of needs, not least the changes of 'label'. The language of 'mental handicap', for example, ceased to be acceptable because it was associated with older perceptions of people so labelled and the automatic 'bad press', stereotypical image Joe Public conjured up on hearing it.

Many people have never had contact with people with severe learning disabilities. Unfortunately what they hear and read in the media often concerns the failures of 'care in the community', rather than its successes. It would seem that we only notice that people that people with disabilities are 'different' when that difference is shown in a negative way, such as someone screaming in a shopping centre. It is like all football supporters being seen as vandals and hooligans, just because the minority who are receive the publicity. Another area of difficulty is the tendency of people to treat adults with disabilities as if they were children. If such people are going to have their gifts recognized and used by the church, such misconceptions need to be acknowledged and overcome.

When we originally looked at starting a group for adults with disabilities in our local church, we organized a series of 'lectures' for those who were interested. They were given by Christian from the caring professions. Our group leaders and some of the helpers were also people who had experience of working in care. Such contact is a useful way to start a group, as our leaders had contacts with homes in the local community and could advertise the existence of the new group.

Our group also became part of the regular Wednesday meetings for Bible study at the church. For the first twenty minutes everyone shares in a joint meeting where we sing a few songs, prayers and a Bible reading. The interaction between members of each group has been invaluable as a way of breaking down barriers of prejudice and misunderstanding, most of which are quite innocent and the result of understandable ignorance on the part of those who have never before had contact with learning disabilities. Then the meeting splits and our large group has its own study, with teaching kept short, enjoyable and fun, which makes learning easier. It soon became apparent that Bible teaching was most effectively done through drama, encouraging maximum participation all round.

It is essential to realize that, like all people from all background, those with learning disabilities are individuals who have their own level of abilities and their own unique gifts and talents. As our drama group has shown, given the right opportunity and encouragement, these people can be used by God to move us all closer to him in wisdom and understanding.

A variety of gifts have been discovered. Michael loves to lead a time of prayer. Margaret comes to the microphone to sing. Philip proved to have a considerable acting talent, while artistic Robert, also an actor, is amazingly creative with costumes and props. Whatever their physical and learning disabilities, these people are not disabled spiritually. The helpers brought their gifts too, those of teachers and musicians, organizers and encouragers.

They realized that some of their acted Bible stories might be performed to the church. No-one had any professional training in drama but the release of God-given gifts within the group carried them along. The whole group became involved in devising their own productions. The whole team talked and prayed it through together. Thus when considering how to present the Good Samaritan, members of the group declined to go in for mugging and eventually suggested an alternative. They substituted a man having an epileptic seizure while out shopping. They knew most people would want to keep their distance. Their unlikely rescuer was a drunken old tramp. They had clearly got Jesus' point.

Soon they found they had a powerful ministry to offer to the wider church and they were in demand up and down the country. Invitations included a Baptist Assembly and the centenary celebrations of the Shaftesbury Society. As the actors mimed their story to a reading from the Bible, their ministry could even cross language barriers: they went on a short mission visit to churches in Poland. Months of planning and rehearsal went into each production. As they presented their gospel dramas, these actors broke down barriers, making people rethink their ideas about disability. They demonstrate that all are given gifts by God to be used to build up each member within the church.

Knowing who is 'crying inside'

Earlier I wrote of the day when Richard alerted us to a woman in the congregation who was 'crying inside'. In a week when devaluing attitudes to people with Down's Syndrome had been in the news, Roy Jenkins spoke of that incident in his 'Thought for the Day' slot on BBC Radio 4. He told me subsequently that none of his talks had netted more correspondence, almost all giving similar examples from up and down the country. Clearly many people whose verbal skills are limited become highly skilled in reading body language and are therefore quick to recognize signs of unhappiness or anxiety. When others learn to respect this, it can be a useful pastoral asset.

Witnesses for Christ

This book has been written out of the experience of daily life with a man who, whatever his impairment of intellect, is a vibrant, joyful Christian. His favourite 'hobby' activity is his private devotions. He will spend long periods in his room preparing his time of worship - choosing a theme and finding appropriate scriptures, prayers, hymns and songs. He has a huge collection of Christian music on CDs and audiotapes - the latter all have to be set at the right place, ready to play the song he wants when he reaches it. When all is ready, Richard has his own private time of worship. Some of the matters for prayer will be those that Christian friends who also have learning disabilities have shared with him. His parents often feel he is the family 'priest', praying on our behalf while we are over-busy about the Lord's work.

I think of many others. Vicki dancing for sheer joy at a BUild conference, Jane playing 'O wonderful love' on her triangle, Verna smiling heavenwards as she completes a Bible reading, Debbie speaking of her baptism, Michael's fervent prayer punctuated with 'Praise the Lord', Dawn teaching others to sign songs of praise, Mark who could 'feel I belong' in the home group, and little Grant peering over the lectern as he sang 'Let the weak say "I am strong"'. Good friends have helped them and many others understand God's love and given them hope and joy in the Gospel, and thus their gifts have been released into the church.

Visiting one church for a 'special needs' weekend, I preached from John 9, so full of those persistent, unhelpful attitudes to disability. At the church door afterwards, a strange thing happened. Almost everyone wanted to tell me or my husband about their experiences of disability, either their own or that of close family. It seemed that a normally locked door had been opened that morning and it was ok, and indeed liberating, to speak of difficult experience. Even in that context I was taken aback when a middle-aged couple came up and the woman, whom I had met on the Saturday, introduced her husband by name, adding 'He has Asperger's Syndrome - [gasp] ooh, I have never introduced him like that before!' 'It's all right', said her husband, and proceeded to tell me what a relief it had been to them both when they had learned the reason for behaviour that they had always known was unusual. Then he excused himself as he had jobs to do for the church.

Disability is part of the human condition, not a rare exception. Society might be a lot healthier if we faced up to how many lives are affected by it, directly or indirectly.

* * * * *

For twenty-five years no day passed when I did not at some point grieve that my younger son had Down's Syndrome. We got on with life with a generally positive outlook, but it was a constant ache in the background.

Then BUild brought the Harlow actors to a Baptist Assembly. On the Sunday morning they re-enacted the passion story. It was, if I remember aright, the first year that the platform proceedings were relayed live on to a large screen. I have never felt the horror of the cross so keenly as when the camera focused on Philip's face, with those familiar Down's features, contorted in agony as the hammer blows rang out. Philip could hardly understand the theology of atonement, certainly his ability to speak of it was limited, but he had grasped the enormity and agony involved. What he had to give he offered fully and entered into the experience of Jesus so powerfully that his face proclaimed the amazing grace of divine love.

For me, seeing Christ with Down's features was a life-changing revelation. Suddenly the pain of Richard's condition left me. As we moved into the communion service that followed I found myself taking trays around with tears on my cheeks. In incarnation Christ had taken on the whole human condition, disability included. From that morning the *pain* of Down's Syndrome left me and that has remained true over the fifteen years since that day.

Some years later, again at Assembly, a fellow member of the BUild committee told me how inadequate he felt on hearing that his friends' new grandchild had Down's Syndrome. 'I find I don't know what to say', he lamented. I called Richard over and asked him. His answer staggered us. 'Tell them it's all right. It's not the end of the world. I don't mind having Down's Syndrome.' Later we heard that this word spoken from real knowledge had indeed helped that family.

The man whom Jesus healed told his questioners, 'One thing I know: once I was blind, now I see.' Once both Richard and his parents hated him having Down's Syndrome. The condition remains but the pain of it has gone, and the agents of healing have been Christ, glimpsed through Down's features, and Christ's body the church, sharing in the pain and loving and valuing the person that Richard is, disability and all.

* * * * *

It is out of such experience, our own and that of many others who live with disability, that this book has been written. Disability exists in God's world but it is not the end of it. The God of grace is Lord, and in Christ weakness itself can be transformed into strength.